PRAISE FOR O'
BY PARIS PERMENTER ᴀɴᴅ ᴊ

Day Trips From San Antonio and Austin

"If you stay in San Antonio for a few days, you don't want to be without a really fine resource book, *Day Trips from San Antonio and Austin.*" –*Family Travel Log*

"*Day Trips from San Antonio and Austin* will be useful to visitors and new residents as well as folks who have been in Central Texas for a while." –*Austin American-Statesman*

"This guide book is good for stashing in the car for those spontaneous Sunday drives or when planning a vacation. Next time family comes to visit, send them a copy of this book before they get here." –*Austin Chronicle*

". . . perfect for those who love to travel, but have limited time, energy and/or budget." –*Johnson City Record Courier*

Texas Barbecue

"This 166-page paperback contains reviews of 96 barbecue joints serving the tastiest brisket, *barbacoa,* and baby backs in the region, as well as smoke-house recipes, festival information, and an ordering guide for barbecue products." –*Texas Monthly*

"If you've ever been in Texas, or plan to visit there, pick up a copy of this blockbuster book." –*RV Today*

"An ideal gift for day-trippers and meat lovers . . ." –*Austin Chronicle*

"Now there's a barbecue guide for out-of-state visitors or natives who want to try a new barbecue place . . . written by a couple of the best Texas writers around . . ." –*Houston Post*

". . . *Texas Barbecue* . . . boasts the beef on the state's best barbecue pits, restaurants, products, cookoffs, festivals, and prize-winning recipes." –*Texas Highways*

The Alamo City Guide

"This book offers practical information about San Antonio and is sensibly divided into areas of town. In addition, you'll get advice about San Antonio's coolest getaways, getting around the city, a diner's guide to Tex-Mex food, as well as a festival overview." –*The Dallas Morning-News*

TEXAS GETAWAYS
for two

PARIS PERMENTER
JOHN BIGLEY

TWO LANE PRESS, INC.

Books by Paris Permenter and John Bigley:
The Alamo City Guide
Day Trips From San Antonio and Austin
Texas Barbecue

First printing April 1996

ISBN: 1-878686 24-0

Printed in the United States of America

Text and cover design: Jim Langford
Maps: Premila Borchardt
Editing: Jane Doyle Guthrie

Although diligent efforts have been made to confirm the accuracy of information contained in this work, neither the publisher nor the authors are responsible for errors or inaccuracies or for changes occurring after publication.

10 9 8 7 6 5 4 3 2 1   96 97 98 99 00

Two Lane Press, Inc.
4245 Walnut Street
Kansas City, MO 64111
(816)531-3119

CONTENTS

Contents

ACKNOWLEDGMENTS

True to its subject matter, the writing of this book has been quite an adventure for the two of us. The journey was frequently made smoother by the support and assistance of our many friends in the Texas travel industry.

We would especially like to thank Molly Alexander of the George-town Convention and Visitors Bureau, Anna Buehrer and Ernie Loeffler of the San Antonio Convention and Visitors Bureau, Cindy Coffner of the South Padre Island Convention and Visitors Bureau, Cathy Dillon of San Marcos's Crystal River Inn, Kim Dillon of the Kerrville Convention and Visitors Bureau, Jana Faber of New Braunfels's Schlitterbahn, Jan and Tracy Hammer of San Antonio's Riverwalk Inn, Marci Ketterer of the Del Rio Chamber of Commerce, Cynthia Maddox of the Texas Renaissance Festival, Donna Mittel of Fredericksburg's Gästehaus Schmidt, Scott Owings and Penni Bentley of the Amarillo Convention and Visitors Council, Judy Ramos of the Arlington Convention and Visitors Bureau, Michael Reeves and Karen Piña of the Lubbock Convention and Visitors Bureau, Victoria Singer de Reyes of the Laredo Convention and Visitors Bureau, and Dana Stephens of the Corpus Christi Area Convention and Visitors Bureau.

On the home front, our thanks go to Lauren Bigley, who helped us research several chapters, as well as to friends and neighbors who "tended the hearth" for us, freeing us to travel: Cliff and Clara Trahan, Tim and Laurie Kibel, Sam Bertron and Rebecca Lowe, and, as always, Paris's parents, Richard and Carlene Permenter.

As with our other guides, this book could not have been produced without the help of publisher Karen Adler, publicist Suzy Chase, office manager Mary Ann Duckers, and editor Jane Doyle Guthrie.

PHOTO CREDITS

We wish to acknowledge and thank the following photo sources: Four
Seasons at Las Colinas (photo on p. 38) and Rockin' R River Rides, New
Braunfels (photo on p. 66).

USING THIS GUIDE

Many destinations in *Texas Getaways for Two* offer urban settings filled with sophistication: fine dining, cultural events, and historic attractions. Others beckon with natural attractions: sun, sand, and surf, cool, damp forests, crisp deserts, or soaring mountains. But Texas is a marriage of both worlds. Regardless of your definition of a romantic getaway—whether it's a sizzling coastal resort or a log cabin tucked in the piney woods, a luxurious spa or a secluded campground, a historic bed-and-breakfast or a high-rise downtown hotel—you'll find many options that fit your fantasy in the Lone Star State.

Selecting a romantic ramble is a job that only a couple can make for themselves, but what we've done is bring together our favorite getaways—as both longtime Texans and a longtime husband and wife team—to offer you a selection of trips to enjoy in a day, over a weekend, or as a longer luxurious vacation.

COST

Within this guide, prices run the gamut, covering attractions and accommodations for every budget. You'll find luxurious spas and elegant resorts favored by celebrities and Texas socialites described alongside modest, low-key getaways where your only cost is some gasoline and a basket of wine and cheese.

Since prices can change as quickly as Texas weather, we've ranked accommodation prices as follows for one night, two adults in a standard room:

$ = under $100
$$ = between $100 and $150
$$$ = over $150

Dining costs per person are indicated as follows:

$ = under $10
$$ = $10 to $15
$$$ = over $15

BED-AND-BREAKFASTS

Just as no one term describes this kind of accommodation, no one set of expectations can be applied to the facilities. Some offer a continental breakfast, others expansive buffets. Some (but not most) permit smoking in guest rooms, others allow it only on the grounds (or not at all). Some treat guests to evening wine and cheese get-togethers, others (mostly private homes offering rooms) prohibit alcohol on the premises.

When booking a reservation, ask questions about minimum stays (often imposed on Friday and Saturday nights in popular destinations), smoking, alcohol, private baths, telephones, breakfast arrangements, and whether children are welcome (pint-size guests are prohibited at many B&Bs to provide a more romantic atmosphere).

For a free brochure listing historic hotels in Texas, including many B&Bs housed in historic homes, write the Historic Accommodations of Texas at P. O. Box 1399, Fredericksburg, TX 78624, or call (210) 997-3980.

VISITING MEXICO

A trip across the border is easy, safe, and fun. In some border cities, the easiest way to enter Mexico is by walking across the International Bridge or Puente Internacional for a small toll. On your return, pay another small toll, walk across the bridge, then head through U.S. Customs.

Every border town has taxi service into and out of Mexico. The ride is only a few dollars each way. Call the local chamber of commerce for information on transportation to Mexican shopping areas or dining spots.

Driving your own vehicle into Mexico can be a somewhat frightening prospect because auto mishaps are a criminal rather than civil offense across the border. (If you're in a wreck, you might find yourself in a Mexican jail, a sure way to spoil a vacation.) Short-term Mexican insurance is required of every driver. Unless you live near the border and carry a special rider on your policy, your car insurance is probably not valid in Mexico. Every Texas border town has several insurance companies that sell short-term Mexican insurance. Call the local chamber of commerce for information on these companies.

Once you're in Mexico, look for secured parking. The larger restaurants have pay parking lots, and these are preferable to parking on the streets.

Remember that Mexican speed signs are posted in kilometers. Also, Mexican traffic lights are slightly different than our own. When you see a yellow light begin to blink, it means that yellow will soon change to red. Mexican streets are very narrow, and often one way, especially in the main tourist areas.

All shopping in the border towns is done with American currency. The "Casa de Cambio" signs are seen on many streets, but you do not need to exchange currency. Most shopkeepers speak fluent English, especially in Nuevo Laredo and Ciudad Acuña. Buying, both in market stores and from street vendors, is usually done by *negociación,* and usually both merchant and shopper part company happy with the deal.

Be careful of counterfeit trademark items, such as $40 Rolex watches sold in many shops. These can be seized, and you must forfeit them if stopped by a customs official.

Heading home, you must cross through U.S. Customs, located on the American side of the International Bridge. The customs official will ask if you are an American citizen. He may ask what you purchased, and he may also ask to see your purchases and other belongings. Certain items, such as fruits, vegetables, animals and birds, and meats (including canned items), cannot be carried back into the United States. Fireworks, switchblade knives (sold by nearly every street vendor), firearms, liquor-filled candy, lottery tickets, and items made from endangered species will be confiscated. Although you can go to the *farmacia* and buy any item without a prescription, you cannot bring it back to the United States.

You must also pass by a booth to pay tax on imported liquor and cigarettes. If you are over 21 years of age, you may bring back one liter of liquor and 200 cigarettes. Texas places a tax on both these items, but the savings are still substantial, especially on items like Mexican beer and tequila.

As far as other goods, you may return with $400 worth of merchandise without paying duty. Every person in your party, regardless of age, has this $400 exemption. If you've made large purchases, save your receipts. You must pay a 10 percent duty on goods over $400 but less than $1,400.

For more information on customs, obtain Publication 512, "Know Before You Go," by writing: U.S. Customs Service, P.O. Box 7407, Washington, DC 20044.

BRIDAL BITS

Throughout this book you'll find special sections featuring some of Texas's most unique wedding sites. We've highlighted historic churches and wedding chapels that are perfect for intimate weddings and vow renewals.

STAYING SAFE AND COMFORTABLE

Nothing puts a damper on romantic notions any faster than sweltering in July humidity or shivering in January under a nylon tent. Contrary to some opinions, Texas has definite seasons. In winter, plan on the possibility of snowy days in the Panhandle, mild to cold days in the central reaches of the state, and comfortable, but not tropical, weather in the far south. In the summer, look for hot days throughout Texas—often topping 100 degrees in many parts of the state by late summer.

While we've made every effort to ensure readers' safe enjoyment of all trips, areas, festivals, activities, and sites included in this book, the areas described vary greatly in the amount of personal preparation necessary for you to have a safe trip. You can make efforts to stay abreast of changing weather conditions, the condition of your automobile and other transportation methods, and the risks associated with recreational activities by considering your personal limitations and the limitations of health, age, and activity level of those traveling with you. Use common sense and good judgment when considering activities, taking into account these factors.

This smorgasbord of 52 excursions, one for every week of the year if you're so inclined, is by no means a definitive list of destinations that make Texans' hearts beat faster. We hope that our search for those hidden spots—the cozy B&Bs, the bluffs with an unbroken view of the sunset, the beach with only two sets of footprints—will continue for us, and for you, for many years to come.

But in the meantime, this book will get you started. It will show you ranches where you can ride horses or savor an African-style safari (complete with an air-conditioned tent at night). It will lead you to small towns where the spirit of the early pioneers still lives on in the traditions, food, and even the language of present-day residents. It will take you to charming lodgings of a bygone era as well as tony city suites, and from picture-perfect picnic spots to first-class gourmet restaurants.

But most of all, it will make you think and view your surroundings like a romantic. As French novelist Marcel Proust put it, "The real voyage of discovery consists not in seeking new landscapes, but in having new eyes."

BED-AND-BREAKFAST GETAWAYS

IF YOU'RE LOOKING FOR A COZY GETAWAY, a chance to overnight in a one-of-a-kind accommodation, then consider a bed-and-breakfast. The term "B&B" covers an array of lodgings: private homes with extra bedrooms, guest homes with no resident owners, and country inns with amenities that might include a small restaurant, tour packages, or a swimming pool.

What B&Bs do have in common is their friendly spirit. Hosts enjoy chatting with guests, recommending area restaurants, and guiding visitors to local attractions. A camaraderie often develops among guests as fellow travelers share tales around an evening fire or at the morning breakfast table.

JEFFERSON
Recommended for: B&Bs, historic homes, shopping

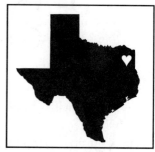

Southern belles. Riverboat captains. Plantation houses. This is Jefferson, a mecca for history buffs and B&B aficionados who want to
spend a few days immersed in the Southern
comfort of East Texas. Here historic homes
offer guests downtown accommodations,
over 40 antique and gift shops tempt travelers, and tours on both land and water provide a look at a community that was once
one of the most thriving commerce centers in Texas.

Over a century ago, Jefferson was known as the "Riverport to the
Southwest." In the 1840s, the town was established as a port city on the
Big Cypress Bayou, linking northeast Texas with Shreveport and the
Red River. Steamers brought supplies and people to Jefferson and left
stocked with the area's richest crop—cotton. At its peak, Jefferson was
the second largest port city in the state. Only Galveston surpassed its
booming business.

After Reconstruction, river traffic started to diminish thanks to the
growing railroad industry. Although it never returned to its earlier status, Jefferson now enjoys a new role: that of the tourist capital of East
Texas. Tucked beneath tall pines and moss-draped cypress trees, this
town now lets visitors step back in time to the heyday of river travel.
Check in a historic B&B, take a river tour, enjoy a mint julep, shop for
antiques, or just walk hand in hand and listen for the echo of a riverboat
steam whistle in the shady bayou country.

A good way to get an overview of Jefferson is on a self-guided walking tour. Stop by the Marion County Chamber of Commerce at 116 W.
Austin Street for a copy of "Historic Jefferson Walking Tours." This
brochure outlines two routes that highlight the historic spots in town.

Both walks begin at the historic **Excelsior House** (211 W. Austin
St., 903-665-2513; $, no ☐). Constructed in the 1850s, this hotel has
been in continuous operation ever since. Built by the captain of the first
steamboat to visit Jefferson, the hotel has seen many famous guests,
including Oscar Wilde, Ulysses S. Grant, Rutherford B. Hayes, and Lady
Bird Johnson. Today you can take a guided tour of the grand hotel or
enjoy a stay in one of its rooms.

Just across the street from the hotel rests the ***Atalanta*** railroad car. Once the private coach of railroad tycoon Jay Gould, the grand 88-foot-long car has four state rooms, a lounge, a dining room, a kitchen, a butler's pantry, and a bath. Today these lavish accommodations, paneled with curly maple and mahogany and filled with original furnishings, are open for daily tours arranged through the Excelsior Hotel.

The walking tour travels past many houses that were built during Jefferson's heyday, mansions with ornate windows and trim. If you're a historic home lover, save time for a guided tour of the **House of the Seasons** (409 S. Alley, 903-665-1218; $$, ☐). Erected in 1872, the house is decorated with period furnishings, and tours include a look at its dome and elaborate frescoes. Besides guided tours, you can also see the place as guests. Three suites are available in the carriage house behind the home, each with whirlpool tubs for two, reproduction Victorian carpeting, TV, and antique furnishings.

You'll also find romantic accommodations throughout Jefferson. Just across the street from the House of the Seasons, the **McKay House** (306 E. Delta, 903-665-7322; $–$$, ☐) offers seven rooms in an 1851 structure.

If you'd rather have more privacy, then head out to **Maison-Bayou Plantation** (300 Bayou St., 903-665-7600; $–$$, ☐). Built on the banks of the bayou, this B&B features accommodations in either a reproduction plantation house or reproduction slave cabins (where you can cozy up in double beds draped with mosquito netting). These rustic structures provide modern comforts like central heat and air and private baths. You'll find plenty to keep the two of you busy at this B&B, including horseback riding, fishing, and hiking.

F Y I ✍

Getting There: Jefferson is located on US 59 in East Texas.

Tours: Home tours of the House of the Seasons are posted daily. For information, call (903) 665-1218. Take a private tour of Jefferson or a romantic evening jaunt aboard Mullins Carriage Service (903-665-2857).

For a look at the bayou that makes Jefferson a port city, take a cruise aboard the *Bayou Queen* (903-665-2222; admission fee). During one-hour tours of Big Cypress Bayou, the captain points out wildlife and Civil War ruins and tells tales of the area's colorful past.

Festivals/Special Events: Grab your costumes and head to Mardi Gras, East Texas–style, in February. Two weekends of street dances, gala balls, and grand parades will have you shouting "Laissez les bon temps rouler!" (903-665-2672).

Home lovers should mark the first weekend in May on their calendars. The Jefferson Historical Pilgrimage, one of Texas's oldest festivals, gives visitors a peek into the elegant homes that make Jefferson special. Hosts dress in period costumes and welcome visitors to these historic residences.

Dining: If you're looking for a taste of the bayou, Jefferson has plenty of restaurants to satisfy your hunger. For oysters on the half shell, catfish, and shrimp, try Oneys (301 N. Polk, 903-665-2211; $$, □). You can dine at a former riverfront warehouse in Auntie Skinner's Riverboat Club (107 W. Austin St., 903-665-7121; $–$$, □). Dine on Southern fried chicken, chicken-fried steak, or chili, then (on Friday and Saturday nights) listen to live music.

The most elegant restaurant in town is the Stillwater Inn (203 E. Broadway, 903-665-8415; $$–$$$, □). Located in an 1890s Victorian home (also a B&B), the restaurant is owned by chef Bill Stewart. Menu selections include steak, seafood, veal, and rack of lamb, accompanied by an extensive wine list.

Jefferson restaurants require membership, purchased for a few dollars, before serving alcoholic beverages.

Bridal Bits: The Maison-Bayou is a popular spot for weddings and receptions, with plenty of room for any size crowd.

For More Information: Call the Marion County Chamber of Commerce at (903) 665-2672.

FREDERICKSBURG
Recommended for: B&Bs, shopping

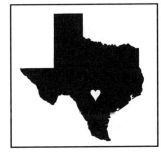

Whether your idea of romance is curling up in front of a fireplace in a secluded log cabin or enjoying a glass of champagne in a whirlpool built for two, Fredericksburg is your kind of place.

This Hill Country town of just over 7,000 residents is the capital city of Texas's burgeoning bed-and-breakfast business. Within Gillespie County, over 200 B&B properties invite guests to enjoy a pampered getaway at prices far lower than those for hotel suites.

Fredericksburg is best known as the home of the *gästehaus,* or guest house, a bed-and-breakfast where visitors enjoy the privacy of their own abode. Unlike traditional bed-and-breakfasts where the owners or managers reside on the premises, guest houses are usually managed by a reservation service. After check-in with the service, guests receive directions and the keys. Often a breakfast, which may range from simple continental to a spread of sausage wraps and homemade pastries, awaits in the refrigerator.

Couples make up a large percentage of the city's overnight guests. "Fredericksburg has really gotten into the romance business," explains Donna Mittel, proprietor of **Gästehaus Schmidt** (210-997-5612; $–$$, □), a reservation service with more than 100 area properties. "Couples are getting away from the kids for the weekend. And we're in a real history-oriented society right now. The interest here in historical properties is unreal."

A popular guest house for couples is **Das Kleine Nest** (210-997-5612; $, □). Every detail of this B&B, from its name (which means "the little nest") to its bedroom loft tucked above a spiral staircase, speaks of romance. Built over a century ago by a hopeful fiancé whose wedding never took place, today this bed-and-breakfast has its own chapel, located behind the home. Whether you come here as a honeymooner or just to enjoy a weekend of romance, you'll find Das Kleine Nest a Lilliputian hideaway, with sleeping quarters that overlook the living and dining area. Rock walls and wood floors as well as antique furnishings recall the home's early days.

One of the most romantically decorated properties in Fredericksburg is Annie's Cabin, one of five guest houses located within the **Austin Street Retreat** (210-997-5612; $, □). The term "cabin" belies the structure's hedonistic accoutrements, such as smoky rose walls that cast a sinful glow on the king-size bed and Cupid's arrow headboard. A whirlpool tub invites couples to share a bubbly retreat beneath a skylight.

Nearby, Kristen's Cabin lures guests into a romantic mood with a king-size bed and a majestic fireplace. The bathroom boasts a two-person whirlpool seated atop a limestone base. Over the years, this room has served as a stable, a dining room, and, in 1885, even a jail. Bars on the windows still recall its role as a cell—today one that only takes two prisoners at a time.

Kristen's Cabin, located just a block from the shopping of Main Street, also gives guests the feeling of quiet seclusion with a private courtyard. Pull up a chair on the limestone terrace and enjoy the sound of a three-tiered fountain playing beneath shady pecans.

Not all guest houses are lavishly styled in the manner of Austin Street Retreat—others are aimed at visitors looking for a simpler country getaway. The **Weber Farmhouse** (210-997-5612; $, □) combines two periods of Fredericksburg's development into one property. This building began as a simple one-room log cabin in the town's earliest days. In 1926, a country Victorian-style farmhouse was constructed around the cabin, completely hiding the original structure. Recently the Delforge family, owners of the popular Delforge Place next door (one of only a handful of traditional bed-and-breakfast homes in town), restored the farmhouse. They stripped down the walls to the original logs and set about giving both the upstairs and downstairs suites a historic theme. The lower rooms recall the days of the stagecoach; the upper guest quarters feature the days of the railroad.

For some travelers, though, romance comes from real seclusion—away from the flurry of town and the temptation of shopping. One remote retreat is the **Schmidt Barn** (210-997-5612; $, □), located one and a half miles from town. Originally a barn, today this 1860s structure is a cozy guest house filled with antiques, a wood-burning stove, and the atmosphere of early Texas. As a further enticement, a Mexican tile tub invites guests to take a leisurely soak. The guest house sits next to the residence of the owners, descendants of some of Fredericksburg's first settlers.

Several guest homes are also available east of town for those seeking country comfort. **Settlers' Crossing** (210-997-5612; $, □), five miles from town, presents a collection of four historic structures located on a 35-acre ranch. Populated by wandering burros and sheep, the ranch is large enough that each guest house affords guests plenty of privacy, whether for an evening stroll or just an afternoon of sipping tea on the front porch.

The Settlers' Crossing guest houses create a peek back into Fredericksburg's past. The Pioneer Homestead, constructed in the 1850s by one of Fredericksburg's first families, brims with period touches, from antique textiles to pine tables to a bedroom ceiling surrounded by intricate stenciling

The nearby Baag Farm House, built in the 1920s as a wedding gift, offers a full kitchen for guests who don't even want to venture from the property for meals. The Indiana House, a log cabin reconstructed on site, holds plenty of period antiques, from its double wedding quilt to the camel back sofa.

But of all the Settlers' Crossing properties, perhaps the most romantic is the Von Heinrich Home. This two-story Pennsylvania Dutch *fachwerk* home was constructed in 1787. Its early days are recalled with folk art, antique rugs, and a Shaker table, and couples can also enjoy a whirlpool tub built for two.

F Y I ✎

Getting There: From Austin, head west on US 290 for 48 miles to the town of Johnson City, and continue west for 30 miles to Fredericksburg. From San Antonio, go north on US 281 to US 290, then turn west and continue for 30 miles.

Nearby Attractions: Wine lovers get ready—this area is home to several excellent wineries. Save time for a tour of Bell Mountain/Oberhellmann Vineyards (TX 16 N. 14 miles from Fredericksburg, 210-685-3297) and Grape Creek Vineyards (between Fredericksburg and Stonewall on US 290, 210-644-2710).

The largest attraction in town is the Admiral Nimitz State Historical Park (340 E. Main St., 210-997-4379; admission fee). Named for Admiral Chester Nimitz, Fredericksburg's most famous resident, the park recalls the life of the World War II commander through displays, the Garden of Peace, and the Pacific History Walk.

For a look at an earlier time in history, visit the Pioneer Museum Complex (309 W. Main St., 210-997-2835; admission fee) to see a

4

24o

collection of typical 19th-century homes, including a "Sunday house." Sunday houses were built by farmers who traveled long distances to do business in town, often staying the weekend.

Shopping: Fredericksburg is a shopper's dream. Regardless of what you're looking for—cowboy kitsch, collectibles, antiques, handmade candles, dulcimers, iron art, one-of-a-kind clothing—you'll find it here. Weekends are busy with day-trippers from San Antonio, who fill Main Street and give the entire downtown a festive atmosphere. You can park and walk to many of the shops.

Dining: Nothing is more romantic than dining outdoors, so if you visit on a pretty day stop for lunch at the Altdorf German Biergarten and Restaurant (301 W. Main St., 210-997-7865; $–$$, □), where the restaurant specializes in German dishes. There's also dining in an adjacent stone building erected by the city's pioneers. For more good German food, also try Friedhelm's Bavarian Inn (W. Main, 210-997-6300; $–$$, □), where we enjoyed some of the best *schnitzel* in the state. One of the most well-known restaurants in Fredericksburg is open for lunch only. The Peach Tree Tea Room (210 S. Adams St., 210-997-9527; $, □) serves up light dishes such as quiche, soup, and salad.

Reservation Services: For reservations at any of these properties, contact Gästehaus Schmidt (231 W. Main, Fredericksburg, TX 78624, 210-997-5612). Other reservation services include Bed and Breakfast of Fredericksburg (619 W. Main, 210-997-4712) and Be My Guest (402 W. Main, 210-997-7227). The Historic Accommodations of Texas is also headquartered in town at P. O. Box 1399, Fredericksburg, TX 78624, or call (210) 997-3980.

Bridal Bits: Adjacent to Das Klein Nest B&B sits Antonette Marie's Wedding Chapel and Social Manor (208 E. San Antonio, 210-997-1753). You can arrive at this quaint chapel by horse-drawn carriage and then enjoy a wedding, vow renewal, or reception for up to 60 people inside or outdoors on the brick-paved patio beneath tall pecan trees.

For More Information: Contact the Fredericksburg Convention and Visitors Bureau at (210) 997-6523.

GEORGETOWN
Recommended for: shopping, small town atmosphere, B&Bs

The Tonkowa Indians were undoubtedly the first promoters of Georgetown. Long before the first survey markers were laid in this Central Texas town, the Indians called this area *takatchue pouetsu,* or "land of good water." No chamber of commerce could have asked for a better slogan. Today that nickname could be expanded. Besides good water, visitors find good recreation, historical sites, and a small town atmosphere that attracts weekend guests.

Georgetown was founded nearly a century and a half ago, and for years the Central Texas town remained quiet, stirring only as shipments of cotton or grains came in from the fields. After the Civil War, however, the railroad, Southwestern University, and the cattle industry came to town, and Georgetown experienced a boom.

The building that occurred during that heyday left Georgetown its legacy of distinctive Victorian architecture. Limestone structures decorated with metal cornices and arched doorways housed businesses that ranged from dry goods and the livery stable to the harness shop. The businesses surrounded a Neoclassical Revival–style county courthouse, forming a typical Texas town square.

From 1982 to 1986, Georgetown participated in the Main Street Project, renovating and rejuvenating historic structures to bring back the look of the 1890s. With the help of the National Trust for Historic Preservation, over $8 million was invested in this project along with $500,000 in improvements including brick pavers, teakwood benches, old-fashioned lighting standards, colorful crepe myrtles, and majestic oaks.

The best way to appreciate the downtown renovation is on a walking tour. Stop by the Visitors Center at 101 W. 7th Street on the square for a brochure outlining a ramble though the town that's been called the "Premier Main Street City of Texas." This self-guided tour takes you throughout the downtown region for a look at the city's most interesting historic sites.

The centerpiece of the square is the **Williamson County Courthouse,** constructed in 1910. It's a classic Texas courthouse, with white

Ionic columns and projecting porticoes. Although it has seen nine decades of change in Williamson County, the courthouse is just an infant compared to many of the neighboring structures. Built in 1870, the Shaffer Saddlery Building, a rubblestone construction at 711 Main Street, was once a saddlery with a residence on the second floor. The west side of the square is also lined with historic structures, including the David Love Building at 706 Austin Avenue. Built in 1883 by settler David Love, the former dry goods store is now a specialty shop popular with visitors. It is believed that the early settler fought at the battle of San Jacinto before he arrived in Georgetown.

Another excellent way to experience historic Georgetown is with a stay in one of its B&B homes. The largest bed-and-breakfast in Georgetown is the **Page House** (1000 Leander Rd., 512-863-8979; $$, □), conveniently located on Interstate 35. This grand Queen Anne–style home dates back to 1903, when it was owned by former gold prospector, rancher, and postmaster J. M. Page. Eventually the grand three-story structure became the property of the Horace M. Weir family. Under their ownership, the house and grounds had their most unique role: home of "Cowboy Polo." The stables became a training center for the cutting horses used as polo ponies in a game identical to the original— but with the addition of cowboy regalia.

Today the training barn has been converted to a meeting center, and the former carriage house now contains guest accommodations. Two rooms offer visitors privacy; four rooms on the second floor of the Page House are for those looking for antique furnishings and historic elegance. Downstairs, the Tea Room offers lunch Tuesday through Saturday from 11 a.m. to 3 p.m. and a three-course dinner on Friday and Saturday nights. Overnight guests start the day with a full country-style breakfast.

One of Georgetown's oldest houses is now a bed-and breakfast. The **Harper-Chessher Historic Inn** (1309 College St., 512-863-4057; $$, □) is listed in the National Registry of Historic Homes. In 1990 the house was completely restored and converted to its present role as an elegant inn. Four rooms with private baths await guests, each room featuring hand-painted murals, antique furnishings, and cutwork linens. Traditional Southern breakfasts are served in the dining room, which is decorated with antique pine furnishings and features one of the six fireplaces within the home. High noon tea with scones and clotted cream is served daily on the veranda. The latter overlooks the garden, a popular spot for weddings and parties.

Also downtown is the **Claibourne House** (912 Forest St., 512-930-3934; $$, □), an elegant Victorian home located three blocks from the courthouse square. Built in 1896, the house was restored in 1987 and converted for use as a bed-and-breakfast inn. Today the grand two-story structure features four bedrooms (with private baths) that are finished with antique furnishings and fine art. Guests can choose from the Periwinkle Room, with its queen-size brass bed and skylighted bath; the Amaryllis Room, with an antique bird's eye maple double bed; the Jasmine Room, with twin iron beds and a fireplace; or the Caladium Room, a downstairs master suite with brass bed and marble bath. Guests at the Claibourne House awaken to a continental breakfast.

As captivating as Georgetown's historic attractions are, some of the area's real treasures are the natural ones. Head north from the courthouse square on Austin Avenue past the North San Gabriel River and turn right to enter **San Gabriel Park.** This community park nestled on the banks of the San Gabriel River has been a popular site for centuries. Indians camped at the verdant grounds, pioneers met here, and early Georgetown residents congregated at the site for parades and meetings, including one where Sam Houston spoke. Today the park is the perfect place to take a picnic lunch and enjoy fishing, swimming, or a leisurely walk on the pecan-shaded grounds.

Upstream from the park, the North San Gabriel River has been controlled to create **Lake Georgetown.** This 1,310-acre lake is located 3-1/2 miles west of Georgetown off FM 2338. Start your visit to the lake with a stop by Lake Georgetown headquarters (west of town off FM 2338; free) to pick up a map to the major park areas. Near the headquarters, pull off for a stop at the Visitors Overlook to see the rugged terrain that forms the lake basin.

Just beyond the overlook lies the first public use area, **Cedar Breaks Park.** Cedar Breaks also has two fishing docks and a boat ramp popular with the many skiers and fishermen who visit the lake.

Cedar Breaks is also the starting point for the **Good Water Trail.** Spanning nearly 17 miles, this hiking trail follows the upper end of the lake, ending at Russell Park on the other side.

One of Georgetown's top attractions is located along (or rather, beneath) Interstate 35. **Inner Space Cavern** (west off I-35, exit 259, 512-863-5545; admission fee) was discovered in 1963 when road crews building the highway drilled into one of the large rooms. For more on the cavern, see "Hill Country Caves" in the "Adventures for Two" chapter of this book.

East of these two attractions lies Southwestern University, the state's first institution of higher learning. Chartered by the Republic of Texas as Rutersville College in 1840, it was moved to Georgetown in 1873 and renamed Southwestern University (after the first choice, "Texas University," was already taken). Its white limestone Cullen Building, built in 1900, is a gem of Texas Victorian style, featuring asymmetrical towers, arches, and turrets. Southwestern gives visitors to Georgetown opportunities far beyond what one would expect from a small town, offering a wide array of cultural and recreational activities. For information, call (512) 863-6511.

Regardless of your interests, from hiking to historic buildings, you'll find it in Georgetown. Best of all, the city greets visitors with a dash of small town charm and a sprinkle of country friendliness, just as it did over a century ago.

F Y I ✍

Getting There: Georgetown is located 30 miles north of Austin on I-35.

Festivals/Special Events: In late March, the fields and yards around Georgetown bloom with the vibrant color of red poppies. Georgetown holds the title of the "Red Poppy Capital of Texas," with both native and cultivated varieties growing throughout the town.

Although the concerted effort of citizens to make Georgetown a poppy showplace is fairly recent, the town's landscape has been brightened by this flower for over 70 years. Many of the poppies date back to seeds imported to the town by Henry Purl "Okra" Compton. During his service in World War I in Europe, he collected seeds and planted them around his mother's home upon his return. Today the poppies brighten yards and highway right-of-ways from late March through May. Look for white signs indicating a "Poppy Zone" as you travel through town.

When spring rolls out its colorful blanket of wildflowers, Georgetown celebrates with MayFair on the Square, held the first weekend of May. This celebration takes place in the historic downtown and highlights the diverse cultures that make this community so special.

December brings a month of celebration to Georgetown. San Gabriel Park twinkles with thousands of tiny lights during the annual Trail of Lights. The Christmas spirit also fills the grand homes featured on the annual Holiday Home Tour. A half dozen residences, all listed on the National Register of Historic Places, open their doors to visitors.

Come in from the cold to warm your hands around a cup of hot cider and take a guided tour of each structure.

Shopping: If there's anything more romantic than the dark recesses of a cavern, perhaps it's a candlelight dinner. Well, you'll have to supply the dinner, but you can certainly stock up on the candles at the Georgetown Candle Factory (located directly across I-35 from Inner Space, 512-863-6025). Owned by Paul and Ellen Nuckolls, this large operation makes hundreds of styles of candles in an assortment of colors, scents, and sizes. The biggest seller is the tiny votive candle, used for everything from lighting *luminarias* to removing the smell of tobacco smoke. You can purchase hand-painted candles, candle arrangements, and ceramic candle holders here as well.

Georgetown is also popular for its many antiques and specialty boutiques along the courthouse square. For a guide to the city's many shops, stop by the Visitors Center for a free brochure.

Dining: For gourmet coffee, stop by Cianfrani Coffee Co. (715 S. Main St., 512-869-7030). Take a deep breath and inhale the richness of freshly ground coffee before enjoying a cup in this shop located in an 1885 building that once housed a saloon and billiards parlor.

Also on the courthouse square, the Courthouse Cafe and Creamery (800 S. Austin Ave., 512-863-9755; $, no ☐) offers sandwiches or a scoop of tempting ice cream. Nearby, El Palacio (806 S. Austin Ave., 512-930-5844; $–$$, ☐) serves Tex-Mex at its best just a block from the courthouse. For rich atmosphere, try the Orient Square Chinese Restaurant (701 S. Main St., 512-863-6104; $$, ☐), where you can dine in elegance in the historic Masonic Lodge.

For More Information: Contact the Georgetown Convention and Visitors Bureau at (512) 930-3545 or (800) GEO-TOWN.

KING WILLIAM HISTORICAL DISTRICT (SAN ANTONIO)
Recommended for: B&Bs, historic homes

Imagine San Antonio without the River Walk. Without the Tower of the Americas. Without the bustling business that fills this modern metropolis.

It is the late 1800s. Texas is still a new frontier, gaining statehood after its years as an independent republic and a territory of Mexico. After years of subsistence on a rugged frontier, San Antonio residents were finally ready for comforts, culture, and a community spirit that emphasized education, music, and the language of their homeland.

With these goals, the King William district began. Started by the founder of the utopian community of Comfort (see the "Cozy Communities" chapter of this book), this elegant neighborhood on the banks of the San Antonio River soon became the home of the city's German community. Here merchants built the city's grandest homes, and this became the preferred address in the Alamo City.

Its status as a superior neighborhood goes back to the mid-1800s, when this district was populated by the Alamo City's most successful businessmen and their families. Many of these frontier citizens were German immigrants with names like Guenther, Wulff, and Heusinger. With their wealth gained in merchandising and investing, they set about building the most lavish homes in the city, most in the grand Victorian style.

For visitors seeking a romantic getaway in San Antonio, a place to enjoy historic elegance in a quiet neighborhood that's within easy walking distance of the River Walk, King William is an ideal destination. Tucked beneath towering live oak trees, this area is home to numerous bed-and-breakfast establishments. Ranging from country comfort to formal elegance, there's a B&B for every taste.

Enjoy an overview of this 37-block area with a walking tour. At the **San Antonio Conservation Society** (107 King William, 210-224-6163), pick up a free brochure that will lead you past grand mansions built in the Neoclassical, Greek Revival, and Queen Anne styles.

One of the most opulent of these residences was the **Steves Homestead** (509 King William St., 210-225-5924; admission fee), positioned right on the banks of the river. Besides a natatorium and a carriage house, the home also boasted the finest furnishings and detail work of its era. Today it's open for public tours, as is the **Guenther House** (205 E. Guenther, 210-227-1061; free) next to Pioneer Flour Mills. Built in 1860, this was the home of Carl Hilmar Guenther, founder of Pioneer Flour Mills. With its crystal chandelier, gold-leaf mirrors, and piano from Stuttgart, Germany, the parlor offers a lovely glimpse of the elegance once enjoyed by the Guenther family. The home's library is now a museum, displaying pieces used by Pioneer Flour throughout the years, from Dresden china anniversary plates to cookie cutters and family photos. The San Antonio River Mill Store is housed in the former music room and bedroom, and visitors can purchase stoneware, baking accessories, and gift items here. Finally, the Guenther House Restaurant, decorated in the Art Nouveau style, serves breakfast, lunch, and Sunday brunch. The old mill still churns out some of the best flour gravy mix found on grocery shelves, along with cornbread, pancake, and similar mixes.

But the best way to enjoy the homes of this neighborhood is as a guest. One of the most unique properties in King William is the **Riverwalk Inn** (329 Old Guilbeau, 800-254-4440; $–$$, □). The inn is located in a two-story log cabin that dates back to the 1840s. Constructed from log cabins brought in from Tennessee, these lodgings recall the atmosphere of San Antonio's earliest days when Tennessee volunteers Davy Crockett and Jim Bowie fought at the nearby Alamo. The inn boasts 11 rooms filled with antique furnishings plus a fireplace, private bath, phone (with voice mail), cable TV, and refrigerator. From its 75-foot porch, rock away your cares and enjoy a glass of lemonade as you watch the activity on the quietest stretch of the River Walk.

For a completely different atmosphere, try the **Ogé House** (209 Washington, 210-223-2353; $$–$$$, □). One of the most elegant B&Bs in town, this 1857 three-story plantation-style home has king and queen rooms filled with antiques. Located directly on the Paseo del Rio, this lovely spot is just minutes away from restaurants and shopping.

You'll also find an authentic historic atmosphere at the **Beckmann Inn and Carriage House** (222 E. Guenther St., 210-229-1449 or 800-945-1449; $$, □). This beautiful home dates back to 1886, when it was built for the daughter of the Guenther flour mill family. Originally this home's address was on Madison Street, but in 1913 the owners decided to extend the front porch around the house on the Guenther Street side. They wanted a new street address, one not shared by a notorious brothel also located on Madison Street at the time! Today this Victorian inn has four guest rooms, each with private baths, and also an adjacent Carriage House with a private entrance.

Another popular King William bed-and-breakfast is **A Yellow Rose of Texas** (229 Madison, 210-229-9903 or 800-950-9903; $–$$, □). The 1878 home has undergone a major renovation and now has an elegant Victorian atmosphere, offering five double rooms with private baths and cable TV.

F Y I ✑

Getting Around: To experience King William in tune with the 19th century, leave your car and travel by trolley. For a quarter fare, hop aboard the Romana Plaza/King William/Blue Star Arts Complex line of the VIA streetcar trolley. This streetcar travels through King William to the Blue Star Arts Complex, La Villita, the Southwest Crafts Center, and the Spanish Governors Palace.

Festivals/Special Events: Organized home tours are conducted annually on the Saturday following Thanksgiving. For tour information, write the King William Association, 1032 S. Alamo St., San Antonio, TX 78210, or call (210) 227-8786.

Shopping: If you're looking for contemporary art, head to the Blue Star Arts Complex (1400 S. Alamo, 210-227-6960). Located on the banks of the river, the complex is a stop on the King William/Blue Star trolley line. The main feature is the 11,000-square-foot Contemporary Art Museum, operated by the artists. Other galleries feature folk art, experimental media, ceramics, and furniture. The Milagros Contemporary Art Gallery displays contemporary art from Latin American, European, and American artists.

Art lovers should also visit the McDaniel Carriage House, built in 1896, now the home of the San Antonio Art League (130 King William St., 210-223-1140; free). Have a look at changing exhibits featuring various types of art, from members' current works to pieces from previous decades.

Dining: Take a quick trip south of the border at Rosario's (1014 S. Alamo, 210-223-1806; $$, ☐). This cafe and cantina is popular with the arts community in King William, but it's equally popular for its specialties: tortilla soup, *enchiladas de mole, chiles rellenos,* and *carne de puerco cascabel* (pork tips in red chile sauce).

Milder fare is the order of the day at the Guenther House Restaurant (205 E. Guenther St., 210-227-1061; $, ☐). This restaurant in the former home of Carl Guenther (founder of Pioneer Flour) features, not too surprisingly, plenty of biscuits and gravy, sweet cream waffles, and pancakes. After a morning of looking at King William's elegant homes, enjoy a light lunch of salad, sandwiches, or soup.

For More Information: Call the San Antonio Convention and Visitors Bureau at (800) 447-3372 for a free visitors packet.

NIGHTLIFE
IN THE BIG CITY

YOU'RE READY FOR AN EVENING OF PARTYING

out on the town. A chance to enjoy a good dinner, then

work it off with some dancing to live music. To stay up

past your bedtime, and enjoy the sights and sounds of the

big city.

Here's a sampling of nightlife, big-city style.

Whether you're looking for the opportunity to do some

boot scootin' to some country music or to dance to alter-

native sounds, you'll find it in Texas. Here's the chance for

the two of you to enjoy an evening of entertainment that

might include a hoedown at the biggest dance hall in

Texas or an intimate blues concert at a smoke-filled bar.

DEEP ELLUM (DALLAS)
Recommended for: nightlife, dining

New Orleans may have its Bourbon Street and Memphis its Beale Street. But Dallas has Deep Ellum.

In a city that's known for its conservative, business-oriented atmosphere, Deep Ellum is sort of the bad boy at school. You remember the one—the kid whose clothes made your parents cringe, who never had a curfew, whose attitude collided with the establishment, and, to tell the truth, the one who always seemed to have the most fun. Well that's Deep Ellum, a neighborhood where the day starts when the sun goes down and the party goes on until the last reveler goes home. When you're in Dallas and you're looking for a night out on the town, this is the place to be.

Deep Ellum may now be the hottest spot in Dallas, the cutting edge of music and art, but its roots extend much further than its current popularity. The neighborhood, now stretching to Commerce and Main Streets, began on Elm Street as a railroad crossing in the 1860s. The area was the home of many blue-collar laborers who, with their Southern drawl, pronounced Elm Street as "Ellum."

Gradually business built up on Elm Street, but the district remained on the fringe of society, a place rampant with prostitution and pawnshops and a general seediness that earned it the nickname "The Bowery of the South."

We first visited Deep Ellum on a hot summer afternoon, a time when the few post-lunch visitors ambled slowly along the vacant streets. The sultry Dallas heat made movement as slow and deliberate as a Texas drawl. But when the sun went down and the lights came on, Deep Ellum showed its exuberance. The sound of glasses clanged from the dark and smoky bars. Cash registers began beeping in the specialty shops. Musicians warmed up for the evening show.

And the party was on. The party goers rolled in, driving everything from Harleys to Jaguars and decked in attire that ranged from black leather to pearls. From every part of the city, people were ready to eat, drink, and be merry for a few hours. From sorority sisters to macho bikers, they were here.

Most came for the music, in clubs like **Club Clearview** (2806 Elm, 214-283-5358), **Club Dada** (2720 Elm, 214-744-3232), and **Trees** (2709 Elm, 214-748-5009), the number one live music venue in Texas according to the Deep Ellum Association. Music has always been the soul of Deep Ellum, the element that elevates this above other entertainment districts that boast road shows and name acts. Deep Ellum features performers from around the country, to be sure, but it also has the distinction of being the place where musicians want to make their start, to make their name, and, in lofts sprinkled throughout the neighborhood, to make their home

Deep Ellum's days as a music capital date back to the 1920s. Blues clubs thrived and recording scouts began prowling the streets looking for talent. Blind Lemon Jefferson, a regular performer in Deep Ellum's brothels, saloons, and streets, was reportedly discovered by a Paramount scout in Deep Ellum, a tin cup in his hand. The best-selling blues musician of his day went on to record classics such as "Bad Luck Blues" and "Hang Man's Blues."

After Blind Lemon's day, Deep Ellum dropped in popularity. The Central Expressway (Interstate 75) was completed in the 1940s and further separated the neighborhood from the downtown. Little by little, the district fell into decline. But in the last 10 years, artists began moving back to the neighborhood, attracted by spacious lofts and inexpensive rent. The area became revitalized as creative residents took warehouses and converted them to storefronts and studios. Others used the warehouses for huge parties, one day realizing that they could open up their own music clubs here.

One of those warehouses was Club Clearview, which opened in 1985 with 10,000 square feet. It brought Deep Ellum back to the forefront of the Dallas music scene. Club Clearview helped give birth to one of Deep Ellum's most famous graduates, Edie Brickell and the New Bohemians, as well as other local musical talents such as Sara Hickman and Vanilla Ice. The club has brought in nationally known names as well, including the Red Hot Chili Peppers, Concrete Blonde, Fishbone, and Chris Isaak.

Operating on a small budget, Club Clearview also offered its walls as a canvas for local artists. Soon the **Art Bar** was born, a corner of Club Clearview that showcases Deep Ellum artists with ever-changing exhibits.

The artists that make Deep Ellum home don't limit their work to clubs and galleries—they have adorned much of the outdoor areas of the district with their work as well. The exterior of Club Clearview, all 6,000 square feet, is adorned with murals. Every Sunday, those murals overlook shoppers in the Club Clearview parking lot. The **Elm Street Market,** a New York–style flea market, takes place every Sunday at this site, offering everything from vintage clothing to one-of-a-kind jewelry.

A year ago, the Deep Ellum Association selected 33 mural artists to paint the walls of the **Good-Latimer Tunnel,** the unofficial "entrance" to Deep Ellum. Each artist, who paid to be able to take part in the project, was assigned a 600-square-foot wall. The result is an eye-catching, highly tailored type of graffiti art that hints at the bohemian atmosphere that defines this neighborhood. On the first Saturday of every October, those murals will be updated, with more art and more landscaping, as part of an annual festival called Tunnel Vision.

FYI

Getting There: Deep Ellum is located east of Central Expressway between the Missouri-Pacific Railroad tracks and I-30.

Festivals/Special Events: In early April, enjoy the Deep Ellum Spring Festival; in early June check out the Deep Ellum Summer Festival. Both offer plenty of live music.

Love Nests: Dallas is well known as the home of some of Texas's most elegant hotels: the Adolphus (1321 Commerce St., 214-742-8200; $$$, □), the Grand Kempinski (15201 Dallas Pkwy., 800-426-3135; $$$, □), Loews Anatole (2201 Stemmons Fwy., 214-748-1200; $$$, □), and the Mansion on Turtle Creek (2821 Turtle Creek Blvd., 214-559-2100; $$$, □). We enjoyed a stay at a more modest historic hotel: the Melrose (3015 Oak Lawn Ave., 800-MELROSE; $–$$, □). Deemed a Dallas Historic Landmark, the renovated hotel has large rooms and a central location.

For More Information: Call (800) C-DALLAS.

RIVER WALK (SAN ANTONIO)
Recommended for: dining, live music, evening strolls

From an open doorway, the sound of dueling pianos, accompanied by the clamor of voices both on- and off-key, fills the street. A few doors down, the sound of *Tejano* hits and the shuffle of dancing feet present an audio invitation for fun. It's a scene witnessed by couples enjoying hand-in-hand strolls down a winding flagstone walk and other visitors cruising the river in open-air barges.

This is the San Antonio River Walk, one of the most romantic sites in a city that's custom-made for lovers. Combining the romance of Mexico with the sophistication of a cosmopolitan metropolis, San Antonio ranks as a top romantic hotspot.

Lovers journey to San Antonio to enjoy its exuberant yet leisurely atmosphere and to let the relaxed attitude of the Mission City soothe their urban blues. While other cities may speed along in the fast lane, San Antonio prefers the scenic route, a perfect pace for the city's many tourists who visit from around the world. Although attractions abound, in this city either a siesta or a tour of a museum is equally acceptable.

Except during the early morning hours, though, expect a fiesta rather than a siesta along the River Walk. The popularity of this site goes back far before the days when people came here for sizzling fajitas and frozen margaritas. The Payaya Indians called this river *Yanaguana,* or "refreshing waters." It also had a less elegant nickname—"a drunken old man going home at night," referring to its numerous twists and turns. Indians camped along the river banks and hunted on the rich land nearby.

In the early 1700s, the Spaniards constructed **missions** on the river's bends. The northernmost site was built first: San Antonio de Valero, later known as the Alamo. Soon settlement began on the riverbanks.

Eventually some of the settlement was less than desirable and the riverside neighborhoods became unfavorable. But the River Walk did not come about until this century. As part of the WPA program, Robert H. H. Hugman was commissioned to develop the scenic walkway. He pictured a festive area he called "The Shops of Aragon and Romula," named for the cities of Old Spain.

Still, development along the River Walk remained minimal until the **World HemisFair.** In the late 1960s, preparing for global visitors, the city beautified the park, investors opened businesses along the walkways, and the River Walk, as visitors today now know and love it, was born.

No matter what day of the week, no matter what time of the year you visit, activity abounds along the River Walk. This is where city residents come to party, where conventioneers come to meet, and where lovers come to taste the flavor that is San Antonio. For the best overview of the 2-1/2-mile River Walk, take a ride on a river barge, a narrated tour that provides a look at stretches most pedestrians never see.

The river winds below numerous bridges (35 in all), each different in style. It flows on past several hotels and finally reaches the floodgates that mark the beginning of the horseshoe bend, the U-shaped section that makes up 50 percent of the walkway but a far greater percentage of the River Walk businesses and visitors. Seventy-five varieties of trees line the walkways—from banana and cypress to colorful crepe myrtle.

But it's at night when the River Walk puts on its most romantic face as the lights shine off the shallow river and sidewalk restaurants illuminate cozy tables with candles. This is the liveliest time at this popular site and you'll find plenty to do, regardless of your musical tastes.

The hottest nightspot on the River Walk is the newly constructed **South Bank.** Until recently, this stretch was generally quiet except for the purr of the river barges and the click of a brew laid on the longest wooden bar in Texas at the Esquire Bar. Today, the South Bank is the liveliest spot on the River Walk. Located across the river from Dick's Last Resort and La Mansion Hotel, this new area is home to **Fat Tuesday's** (111 W. Crockett, 210-212-7886), a frozen daiquiri bar billing itself as "a loosely organized street party" that brings the atmosphere of the Big Easy to San Antonio, and **Howl at the Moon** (111 W. Crockett, 210-212-4695), a sing-along bar that features dueling pianos. Not for quiet types, this place is filled with folks singing along to show tunes and classic rock 'n' roll songs.

Popular around the globe, San Antonio now has its own **Hard Rock Cafe** (111 Crockett St., 210-224-7625; $$, ☐). Part of the new South Bank development project, the Hard Rock is filled with rock 'n' roll memorabilia, good old American food, and, of course, the popular Hard Rock Cafe gift shop selling the requisite T-shirts. The Hard Rock has now been joined by **Planet Hollywood** (245 E. Commerce, 210-212-7827; $–$$, ☐), a restaurant that features movie memorabilia.

Jazz lovers should immediately head to **Jim Cullum's Landing** (123 Losoya at the Hyatt Regency Hotel, 210-223-7266). Jim Cullum and his jazz band play New Orleans–style Dixieland several nights a week. You'll also find Dixieland as well as traditional jazz at **Dick's Last Resort** (406 Navarro St., 210-224-0026), a restaurant that features many local performers.

A lot of folks look for a hole-in-the-wall kind of place when they visit a city. That's not easy to find along the River Walk, but the closest you'll come is the **Esquire Bar** (155 E. Commerce St., 210-225-2521). Located on the north bend of the River Walk, just past the floodgates, this joint has been a San Antonio watering hole since 1933. The smoke-filled tavern is dominated by the original bar.

For laughs, you might try the **River Center Comedy Club** (849 E. Commerce in the Rivercenter Mall, 210-229-1420), which features both San Antonio's top comics and nationally known comedians. A favorite with locals and visitors alike, reservations are recommended.

If you'd rather dine before hitting these hot nightspots, you'll find plenty of restaurants along the River Walk. Stop by the **Texas Tamale Company** (111 W. Crockett St., 210-225-7699; $, □), a Houston-based Mexican deli, for tamales stuffed with everything from cheese to cinnamon. If it's barbecue you're craving, **The County Line** (111 Crockett St., 210-229-1941; $$, □) is an institution among Texas barbecue lovers. Like its other locations around the state, this County Line specializes in an all-you-can-eat extravaganza where you'll feast on beef ribs, brisket, and sausage.

Ask many San Antonians for their favorite River Walk eatery and you'll hear the name Boudro's (421 River Walk, 210-224-8484; $$, ʾ). This steak and seafood restaurant offers the finest in Southwestern cuisine, usually with a twist that makes it unique even among San Antonio's plethora of excellent eateries. Start with a cactus margarita, a frozen concoction highlighted with a jolt of red cactus liqueur. Follow that eye-opener with an appetizer of smoked chicken or crab quesadillas or crab and shrimp tamales. Save room, though, for Boudro's specialties—coconut shrimp, pecan-grilled fish fillet, or the specialty of the house, blackened prime rib. Seating is available along the River Walk or in the dining room.

Another popular local favorite is the **Zuni Bar and Grill** (511 River Walk, 210-227-0864; $$, □). This restaurant also serves Southwestern cuisine to River Walk diners, with selections that start with blue corn nachos and andouille and brie quesadillas and then progress to specials such as roasted poblano peppers filled with shrimp and mozzarella and spicy fajitas served with black beans.

The River Walk's most romantic dining is found at **Little Rhein Steakhouse** (231 S. Alamo, 210-225-2111; $-$$, □). Located where La Villita meets the River Walk near the Arneson River Theatre, this restaurant offers an excellent selection of fine steaks and serves diners at candlelit tables on terraces overlooking the river. On less pleasant days, you may choose to dine inside this historic steak house (built in 1847), which witnessed the development of San Antonio under six flags. The stone building also survived the battle of the Alamo only a few blocks away. From the extensive menu here you can choose anything from T-bone to rib eye to porterhouse steak, all served with Texas caviar, a mixture of black-eyed peas and chopped onion. Reservations are recommended.

If it's a really special occasion, look to the most elegant and pricey restaurant near the River Walk (and indeed in the city). The *prix fixe* menu at **The Fig Tree** (515 Paseo De La Villita, 210-224-1976; $$$, □) features continental cuisine, including beef Wellington, lobster, and rack of lamb, as well as buffalo rib eye, venison and antelope tenderloins, and quail. This restaurant is open for dinner only, and reservations are recommended.

But don't spend all your time on the River Walk dining. Budget some time for another favorite River Walk sport: shopping. Small boutique shops feature Texas-made products, Mexican imports, art, and clothing. For a shopping blow-out, head to the **Rivercenter Mall,** located on a man-made arm of the River Walk specially constructed to link the shopping center with the popular tourist destination. With aqua-tinted windows and a U-shape construction that surrounds an arm of the river, Rivercenter is more than your typical mall.

The most unique River Walk shopping is found in **La Villita.** This historic site, the first permanent settlement in San Antonio, is today filled with art galleries, studios, and import stores.

F Y I ✎

Getting There: The River Walk area is located downtown.

Festivals/Special Events: Every visitor feels romantic during the holiday season, when Fiesta de las Luminarias illuminates the River Walk with thousands of little candles in sand-weighted paper bags. During the Holiday River Festival, the River Walk is transformed into a Christmas wonderland with hundreds of thousands of tiny lights. On the lighting night following Thanksgiving, the river hosts a floating parade. But the most moving event is Las Posadas, a beautiful ceremony dramatizing Joseph and Mary's search for an inn, with costumed children leading a procession down the River Walk. Holiday songs ring out in both English and Spanish.

Love Nests: Some of the most romantic accommodations on the River Walk are found beyond the stretch that most pedestrians reach. King William, a historic neighborhood located on the southernmost reaches of the River Walk, is home to many elegant B&B properties, some located directly on the river. (For more information, read about this area in the "Bed-and-Breakfast Getaways" chapter of this book.)

Directly on the River Walk, you'll find some of the nicest and priciest rooms in the city. Near South Bank, La Mansion del Rio (112 College St., 210-225-2581 or 800-531-7208; $$$, ☐) is housed in an elegant Spanish-colonial-style structure that began as the St. Mary's Academy in 1854. Today the hotel has 337 rooms and suites, many with private balconies overlooking the River Walk.

Continuing south, you'll reach one of the crown jewels along the River Walk, the Hyatt Regency San Antonio (123 Losoya St., 210-222-1234 or 800-233-1234; $$$, ☐). This hotel is located on the bend in the river and it captures all the excitement of the Paseo del Rio. Whether you enter from the street or the River Walk, you'll admire the soaring atrium filled with palms and the sounds of falling water. Glass elevators whisk guests to the 631 rooms above.

Near the Rivercenter Mall, couples can select from two Marriott hotels. The original property was the Marriott Riverwalk (711 E. River Walk, 210-224-4555 or 800-228-9290; $$$, ☐). Built in 1979, the 500-room hotel is located directly between the mall and the convention center. Just steps away, the newest Marriott is the Marriott Rivercenter (101 Bowie St., 210-223-1000 or 800-228-9290; $$$, ☐). This 1,000-room establishment soars from the Rivercenter Mall, looming over the River Walk above any other downtown hotel. The hotel boasts an executive health club with indoor and outdoor pools, hydrotherapy pool, saunas, and exercise equipment to use if you feel like too many Tex-Mex dinners are slowing you down.

Further south stands the Hilton Palacio del Rio (200 S. Alamo St., 210-222-1400 or 800-HILTONS; $$$, ☐). The hotel has a wonderful location, right in the middle of the River Walk action and just a few short steps away from La Villita and HemisFair Plaza.

And, if you're looking for ultra luxury (à la Donald Trump), you can have the run of the house at the Lone Star Palace (321 Alamo Plaza, 210-531-2323; $$$, ☐). Directly across from the Alamo, this penthouse includes two bedrooms, three baths, a sitting room, a living room, and a kitchen, all decorated in true Texas style, plus a patio and rooftop terrace where you'll enjoy the city's best view of the Alamo.

Available for groups as large as 200 (perfect for a wedding and reception), this downtown hideaway is also available as an overnight suite with concierge service and continental breakfast. (Catering is available through the Hyatt Regency San Antonio, which also handles reservations for the unique getaway.) Romantic packages can include such luxuries as chilled champagne, gourmet dinner for two on the terrace, breakfast in bed, a hot air balloon ride across San Antonio, a sunset carriage ride, a moonlight ride on a River Walk barge, or a limo tour of the Alamo City. Be warned: Such luxury comes at a hefty price. If you have to ask, you probably can't afford this hideaway.

For More Information: Call the San Antonio Convention and Visitors Bureau at (800) 447-3372 for a free visitors packet. When you get in town, the best source of information is the Visitor Information Center (317 Alamo Plaza), operated by the San Antonio Convention and Visitors Bureau. The center sits directly across from the Alamo.

SIXTH STREET (AUSTIN)
Recommended for: live music, dining

Austin calls itself the "Music Capital of the World." On any given night, you'll find clubs pulsating to the rhythm of blues, country, rock, and alternative sounds.

Television viewers around the nation are familiar with Austin's music scene because of *Austin City Limits,* a show taped on the campus of the University of Texas. For information on tickets to the show,  which is taped from August through February, call (512) 475-9077.

The legacy of Austin's music scene is one passed down by greats such as the late Stevie Ray Vaughn, Janis Joplin, Willie Nelson, Jerry Jeff

Walker, and others who have drawn the attention of the music world to this corner of Texas. In venues that range from the 17,800-seat **Frank Erwin Center** (1701 Red River, 512-477-6060 for tickets) on the University of Texas campus to the crowded smoke-filled clubs, the city is alive with the sounds of big-name performers and yet-to-be-discovered hopefuls.

Much of the action revolves around Sixth Street, the east-west thoroughfare tucked between the State Capitol and Town Lake. It may only be a short walk from the seat of state government, but, make no mistake, this is a district where the emphasis is on fun. Nightclubs and restaurants tempt the steady pedestrian stream with blaring music, exotic drinks, and some of the best dining in the River City.

Although you'll find live music throughout Austin, from blues at **Antone's** (2915 Guadalupe, 512-474-5314) to country and western at the **Broken Spoke** (3201 S. Lamar Blvd., 512-442-6189), the pulse of the music scene is best felt on Sixth Street, where the party starts late and continues until the early hours.

Sixth Street is one of the first introductions many visitors get to Austin, but it's just as popular with residents. Friday and Saturday nights are often standing room only in an entertainment district that's sometimes compared to New Orleans's Bourbon Street. Here blues, rather than jazz, is king, and it's found in little clubs like **Joe's Generic Bar** (315 E. 6th St., 512-480-0171), **Maggie Mae's** (512 Trinity, 512-478-8541), and the **311 Club** (311 E. 6th St., 512-477-1630).

The Sixth Street area is also home to several local brew pubs, including the **Copper Tank Brewing Company** (502 Trinity St., 512-478-8444), with five beer choices daily. This large brew pub has a 90-foot mahogany bar and space for banquets as large as 600 persons.

Austin has many romantic features, but one of its most romantic dates back to 1885. This was the advent of "artificial moonlight," which bathed the city in an evening glow disbursed by 27 tall towers sprinkled throughout town. Today just a few of these **moonlight towers** remain (head to the intersection of 9th and Guadalupe to smooch beneath the false lunar glow).

F Y I

Getting There: Sixth Street is located in downtown Austin. Traffic on the one-way street runs east to west, and parking can be extremely limited. Your best bet is to look for parking in the lots north and south of Sixth.

Festivals/Special Events: A Halloween party takes place on Sixth Street, complete with 20,000 to 70,000 merrymakers. This is one of the largest Halloween celebrations in the nation, and the street is closed to all but pedestrian traffic. You'll see every imaginable sort of costume here, plus a few you never could have imagined.

In addition, clubs up and down Sixth Street (plus others throughout the city) feature groups from around the country during South by Southwest Music and Media Conference in mid-March. (512) 467-7979.

Dining: Dining is never a problem on Sixth Street; you name it, you'll find it. A longtime favorite is Dan McKlusky's Restaurant (301 E. 6th St., 512-473-8924; $$$, □), serving steaks and seafood in the heart of Sixth Street. You'll also find elegant dining at the Old Pecan Street Cafe (310 E. 6th St., 512-478-2491; $$$, □). This cafe, echoing the original name of Sixth Street, is a popular location for wedding receptions, with rooms that can seat up to 300 guests.

For Cajun food, try Fat Tuesday's (508 E. 6th St., 512-474-0632; $–$$, □), or, whenever you get hungry, head down to the 24-hour restaurant Katz's Deli and Bar (618 W. 6th, 512-472-2037; $–$$, □).

Love Nests: There's no contest as to Sixth Street's most romantic lodgings—the winner is clearly the Driskill Hotel (112 E. 6th St., 800-252-9367 or 512-474-5911; $$$, □). Built in 1886 by cattle baron Jesse Driskill, this is Austin's oldest hotel. Its 177 rooms and beautiful lobby recall an elegant age in the city's history. The hotel sits within easy walking distance of the State Capitol and the Sixth Street entertainment district. Two restaurants and bars offer food and refreshments to guests preferring to "stay in."

For More Information: Contact the Austin Convention and Visitors Bureau at (800) 888-8287. While in town, stop by the Visitors Information Center at 201 E. Second Street.

STOCKYARDS (FORT WORTH)

Recommended for: country music and dancing, train ride, B&Bs

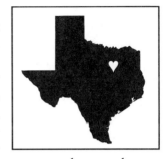

Pick up your cowboy hat, pull on your boots, and grab your partner. It's time to party, Fort Worth–style. If you're looking for a chance to dress like a cowboy, do a little line dancing, or ride the mechanical bull, here's your opportunity. Fort Worth is a city that parties in style, and that style is true country and western. Nowhere is the "kick up your boot-heels" spirit more evident than in the Stock-yards. This National Historic District is still home to cowboys on horse-back as well as historic hotels, Western shopping, and the city's top nightlife.

Formerly the Stockyards were known as the biggest hog and sheep marketing center in the Southwest. Here, too, cattle once filled Exchange Avenue, traded like stock in The Livestock Exchange, formerly called "The Wall Street of the West." Today the flavor of the livestock exchange lives on through sites such as the **Cowtown Coliseum** (121 E. Exchange Ave., 817-625-1025), built in 1908. The building still is home to professional rodeos held every Saturday night from April through September.

Probably the best known attraction in the Stockyards is **Billy Bob's Texas** (2520 Rodeo Plaza, 817-624-7117). Billed as the "World's Largest Honky-Tonk," this Texas-sized nightclub spans 100,000 square feet with 40 bar stations, live bull riding, and an arena for 6,000 guests to enjoy top performers. Big names in the country world have performed at Billy Bob's, from Garth Brooks to Clint Black to Tanya Tucker. You can visit a hallway featuring cement impressions of every performer's hands and autograph. Even if a top performer is not playing at Billy Bob's, you'll find plenty to do. The indoor arena here is home to shows every weekend as professional riders try to stay on bucking bulls.

You'll find plenty of other nightlife in the Stockyards district, too. Stop by the well-known **White Elephant Saloon and Beer Garden** (106 E. Exchange Ave., 817-624-1887) for live country and western music every day, the **Rodeo Exchange** (221 W. Exchange Ave., 817-626-0181) for country dance lessons on Tuesday and Wednesdays, or

The Cantina (124 W. Exchange Ave., 817-740-1288) for rodeo videos and a real Western decor.

While you're in the Stockyards, check out the ***Tarantula Train*** (Stockyards Station Market at 140 E. Exchange Ave., 800-952-5717; fee). This 1896 steam locomotive takes passengers on a nostalgic ride through 10 miles of historic Fort Worth. (Don't worry—there are no tarantulas on the train. The strange moniker grew from a map drawn of early Fort Worth. The wiggly rail lines that led into the heart of the city reminded someone of spider legs, hence the name.) You can also depart from the station on a luxury ride to nearby Granbury on a train decorated in 1940s style, complete with a glass-dome car and fully stocked bars.

F Y I ✍

Getting There: The Stockyards are located 2-1/2 miles north of downtown Fort Worth just off Interstate 35 West and Interstate 20. Most of the action is found along Exchange Avenue and Stockyards Boulevard, which run east-west off North Main Street.

Festivals/Special Events: The Fort Worth Stockyards National Historic District kicks up its heels all through the year at events such as the Chisholm Trail Round-Up in June, Pioneer Days in September, Red Steagall's Cowboy Gathering and Western Swing Music in October, and Christmas in the Stockyards during the holiday season.

Shopping: Here's your chance to dude up like a cowboy with authentic boots, a hat, and other Western gear. You'll find shops all along Exchange Avenue featuring everything from souvenirs to saddles. The most complete collection of stores cluster in the Stockyards Station Market (140 E. Exchange Ave., 817-625-9715), where nearly two dozen specialty shops sell Western art, leatherwork, jewelry, collectibles, souvenirs, and more. Another excellent stop is Maverick Fine Western Wear (100 E. Exchange Ave., 817-626-1129). Built in 1905 as a hotel, through the years the building has housed a bordello, a gambling hall, and a social club. Today the renovated structure is packed with clothing, jewelry, and gifts, and you can even belly up to the bar, order a longneck, and shop in true Western fashion.

Dining: All that two-steppin' can work up an appetite, and you'll find plenty of places to fill up throughout the Stockyards. Naturally, beef rules, and you'll find it at Risky's Barbecue (Stockyards Station Market at 140 E. Exchange Ave., 817-626-7777; $–$$, □), the Cattleman's Steak House (2418 N. Main St., 817-624-3945; $$–$$$, □), and The Feedbag (140 E. Exchange Ave., 817-626-6660; $$–$$$, □). For Tex-Mex, Joe T. Garcia's (2201 N. Commerce St., 817-626-4356; $$, □) is legendary (get there early–this is a very popular place for both indoor and outdoor dining). If it's Italian you're looking for, Spaghetti Warehouse (600 E. Exchange Ave., 817-625-8586; $$, □) offers quiet dining and ever-favorite dishes such lasagna and many varieties of spaghetti.

Love Nests: The Stockyards Hotel (109 E. Exchange Ave., 800-423-8471; $, □) is known as the place Bonnie and Clyde slept. Dating back to the turn of the century, this historic hotel is a Stockyards favorite. It's also the home of Booger Red's (817-625-6427; $–$$, □), a restaurant named after a oddly monikered cowboy.

Bed-and-breakfast lovers shouldn't miss Miss Molly's B&B (109-1/2 W. Exchange Ave., 800-996-6559; $–$$, □). With eight rooms, this historic hotel was once a brothel and recalls its bawdy history with Miss Josie's Room (where a bathtub stands on a platform overlooking the room). The rooms are furnished in 1920s style, complete with iron beds.

For More Information: Call the Fort Worth Convention and Visitors Bureau at (800) 433-5747.

RICHMOND AVENUE (HOUSTON)
Recommended for: live music, dining, shopping

If you're ready for entertainment big city–style, then head to Houston. Nowhere else in Texas will you find such a vast selection of nightlife, tempered with fine dining and world-class shopping. The nation's fourth largest city, Houston is a sprawling mix of cultures, with funky neighborhoods that offer music to suit any taste.

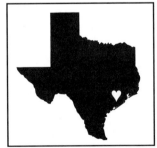

The trendiest place in Houston is undoubtedly the **Richmond Avenue Entertainment District** (713-974-4686). Located near the **Galleria** (a veritable mecca for die-hard shoppers), Richmond Avenue boasts a mix of entertainments as well as dining, brew pubs, and a general party atmosphere. Most clubs are found in the stretch of Richmond that extends from the 5600 block to the 6500 block.

One of the most popular (and certainly the easiest to spot) clubs is the **Billy Blues Bar and Grill** (6025 Richmond Ave., 713-266-9294), part of a San Antonio–based chain. What makes this location stand out is the "Smokesax," a 63-foot statue that's the creation of artist Bob "Daddy-O" Wade. Commemorating Houston's history of R&B, this work holds the distinction of being the world's largest saxophone sculpture. The sculpture is built on a Volkswagen chassis and sports a surfboard for a reed. Since, after all, this is a barbecue joint, the Smokesax blows real smoke. Pecan-smoked barbecue is the order of the day here, and every night this popular eatery hosts some musicians, primarily of the blues persuasion.

You'll also find R&B as well as other types of music at **City Streets** (5078 Richmond Ave., 713-840-8555), where six clubs with completely different themes entertain guests of all musical persuasions.

Dance is the number one attraction of **Club Blue Planet** (6367 Richmond Ave., 713-978-5913), a Top 40 dance club that features nationally touring acts. The action occurs around the pool tables, shuffleboard courts, and midway at **Dave and Buster's** (6010 Richmond Ave., 713-952-2233.)

Nightclubs go hand in hand with restaurants, and you'll find plenty of those along Richmond Avenue as well. Stop by the **Trail Dust Steak House** (6100 Richmond Ave., 713-266-0656; $$–$$$, □) for Texas-sized steaks, ribs, and more. After dinner, work off that beef with some country-and-western dancing to live music. You'll also find steaks served in an elegant atmosphere at **Ruth's Chris Steak House** (6213 Richmond Ave., 713-789-2333; $$$, □).

For something a little more exotic, consider **Sammy's Lebanese Restaurant** (5825 Richmond Ave., 713-780-0065; $$–$$$, □), serving up everything from *falafels* to *tabouli.*

If it's Tex-Mex you're hankering for, Richmond Avenue also serves up plenty of spicy dishes. **Chuy's** (6328 Richmond Ave., 713-974-2322; $$, □) offers everything from green chicken enchiladas to *chalupas* and mixes some killer margaritas. **Pappasito's Cantina** (6445 Richmond Ave., 713-784-5253; $$–$$$, □) is known as a slightly more upscale Tex-Mex joint (where lines can be long, so come early).

For seafood, don't miss **Joe's Crab Shack** (6218 Richmond Ave., 713-952-5400; $$–$$$, □), a funky restaurant with a rustic decor and outdoor dining on fresh catch.

F Y I 〜

Getting There: The Richmond Avenue area is located in uptown Houston near the Galleria (7 miles from downtown Houston, 27 miles from Houston Intercontinental Airport).

Festivals/Special Events: Throughout the year, Houston is alive with festivals. One of the largest is February's Houston Livestock Show and Rodeo, a 17-day party with lots of live country-and-western music as well as traditional rodeo events. In April, enjoy Worldfest, an international film festival, followed in August by the Houston International Jazz Festival celebrating the birth of jazz.

Shopping: The number one shopping spot in downtown Houston is the Galleria (5075 Westheimer, 713-621-1907). The sprawling mall boasts over 300 shops, including Neiman-Marcus, Marshall Fields, Lord and Taylor, and Macy's. After a few hours of shopping, enjoy some ice skating on the indoor rink or catch a film at one of four theaters.

Love Nests: Houston is filled with luxury hotels that can make any weekend a special event. If you'll be shopping at the Galleria or enjoying nightlife along Richmond Avenue, two Westin hotels are located right in the Galleria complex. The Westin Galleria and the Westin Oaks (5060 W. Alabama, 800-228-3000; $$–$$$, ☐) both rise up out of the uptown mall complex. The Galleria property has 485 rooms; the Westin Oaks is slightly smaller, with 406 rooms. All the rooms in both properties have private balconies, voice mail message systems, and access to heated outdoor swimming pools, tennis courts, a putting green, and a jogging track—as well as the facilities within the Galleria itself.

Five minutes from the Galleria, the Houston Medallion (3000 North Loop West, 800-688-3000; $$–$$$, ☐) has 382 rooms, including four stories set aside for luxurious concierge service with key-card access only, complimentary continental breakfast, afternoon hors d'oeuvres, and late night desserts. The hotel is decorated with Native American artifacts and a Southwest theme that carries over into the Cimarron Restaurant, which features regional ingredients and Southwest cuisine.

For More Information: Call the Houston Convention and Visitors Bureau at (800) 4-HOUSTON.

PURE LUXURY

SOMETIMES THERE'S NO GREATER LUXURY than the opportunity to be pampered. Whether at the hands of a skillful masseuse or a gourmet chef, these hedonistic destinations can provide the best life has to offer.

FOUR SEASONS AT LAS COLINAS
Recommended for: luxury, golfing, spa facilities, dining

Even J. R. Ewing never had it so good. Evian spritzers and chilled towels to cool tanning skin. Mornings spent on a championship golf course followed by afternoons in a luxurious spa and a pampering salon. A limo ride to Neiman-Marcus to be greeted by a personal shopping assistant.

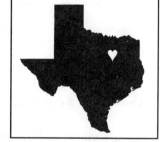

Thanks to the long-running television series, the Dallas–Fort Worth Metroplex has an image as a place of luxury and wealth where the ultra-rich can enjoy the finest in life. But even oil barons would have a hard time topping the pampered lifestyle enjoyed, even if only for a brief visit, by guests at the Four Seasons at Las Colinas (4150 MacArthur Blvd., 214-717-0700 or 800-332-3442; $$$, ☐).

Las Colinas, Spanish for "the hills," is a planned community in the city of Irving just west of the Dallas skyline. It boasts some of the largest businesses in the world, companies like Exxon, GTE, and Sprint. To accommodate the executives that shuttle in and out of Las Colinas, the Four Seasons was built in 1986. CEOs can wind down with 18 holes of golf, a game of tennis or squash, or perhaps a relaxing Swedish massage followed by a world-class meal. The resort has been named by *Conde Nast Traveler* as one of the top 10 hotels in the United States and one of the top 100 in the world.

Now couples looking for a weekend of pampered luxury are also enjoying the full-service resort. Here days stretch from breakfast served on your balcony overlooking the 400-acre resort to some late evening relaxation in the bubbling hot tub where steam rises from a flowing waterfall made of natural stone. Whether it's languid luxury or nonstop activity you're seeking in a weekend away, it can probably be found at this resort.

For many guests, activity means golf at the **18-hole championship course.** The course winds behind the resort, with views of the hotel, Irving's high-rise executive towers, and the gently rolling prairie. Couples often enjoy a round of twilight golf on this course, carrying chilled champagne and caviar in their cart for a romantic twist on the sport.

It's all business on the course, however, during the GTE Byron Nelson Classic, a PGA tour event that draws over 20,000 onlookers. This event occurs every May. The Tournament Players Course begins at a 9-foot bronze statue of Byron Nelson, the octogenarian championship golfer who still frequently plays the course. His PGA gold medals and other memorabilia from his unmatched career are displayed in the **Sports Club,** a 176,000-square-foot facility used by both resort guests and club members.

Activities here at the club include racquetball, squash, indoor and outdoor tennis, half-court basketball, swimming in heated pools, jogging on indoor and outdoor tracks, over 50 exercise classes weekly, and workouts in a full fitness center. And if you're looking for a good excuse not to exercise, don't plan to just leave your workout clothes and shoes at home. The club offers complimentary use of full workout gear.

If your workout wakes up some long-forgotten muscles, make your next stop **The Spa.** Separate men's and women's sections pamper guests in a luxurious environment. Cocoon yourself in an oversized terry robe, enjoy a glass of iced spring water, then relax in the steam room, sauna, or whirlpool. An invigorating cold plunge pool is also available.

Massage—Swedish, Shiatsu, and aromatherapy—is one of the most requested treatments at the Spa, performed by licensed therapists. Couples can even request a special double room to enjoy their massages together. All treatments, from herbal wraps to the loofah salt glow, are designed to leave guests feeling refreshed and pampered.

With its attention to health and fitness, it's natural that the resort would also pay special notice to diet. **Nutritional counseling** is available in the Sports Club, but even casual diners can select a healthy meal by looking for "Alternative Cuisine" starred on the Four Seasons menus. These healthy entrees, low in fat and cholesterol, are served in even the resort's toniest restaurant, **Cafe on the Green.** Diners can leave jackets and ties back in the room, but still enjoy classic service in the elegant but not stuffy atmosphere.

Although this resort offers plenty of activities to keep guests busy, you'll also find attractions just minutes away. The hotel and **Neiman-Marcus** have a special arrangement for guests. You can pick up a certificate from the concierge and arrange for transportation in the house Town Car (on a space available basis) to the flagship store. Upon arrival, you'll be greeted by a personal shopper, receive a silver photo frame, and enjoy browsing in the store whose name is synonymous with Texas elegance.

But don't crowd too much activity into your weekend away. Guests lounging around one of the Four Seasons's three pools, soaking in the hot tub, or just sitting on their balconies enjoying a North Texas sunset know one thing: Sometimes the biggest luxury is just the luxury of being able to do nothing at all.

F Y I ❧

Getting There: Irving is located on the northwest side of Dallas. In Dallas, take Loop 12 west to the city of Irving. The Four Seasons at Las Colinas is located at 4150 North MacArthur Boulevard. The resort is 15 minutes from the Dallas–Fort Worth International Airport and about 20 minutes from Love Field.

Nearby Attractions: The city of Irving also boasts plenty of distractions for weekend visitors. Texas Stadium (214-438-7676), home of the Dallas Cowboys, is located only minutes away from the resort. Even if the team is not in town, you can enjoy a one-hour guided tour of the facility. Next door, the Starcenter Ice Arena (214-831-2400) is home of the local National Hockey League franchise, the Dallas Stars.

You'll also see stars, or at least displays about them, at The Studios at Las Colinas (214-869-FILM). Movies like *JFK, Robocop,* and *Problem Child* have used these production facilities. Tour the studios for a behind-the-scenes look at the soundstages, dressing rooms, lighting departments, production offices, and a special effects studio used to create many of the frightening looks used in familiar films. Movie memorabilia is also on display.

The best known symbols of Irving are the Mustangs of Las Colinas, nine steeds captured in bronze and frozen in mid-gallop. The Mustangs are located near another symbol of Irving: the Mandalay Canal. Like a smaller version of the San Antonio River Walk, the Canal is located below street level and lined with specialty shops and outdoor dining. Venetian water taxis transport visitors along the canal.

For More Information: For more on the resort, call (214) 717-0700. For more on Irving attractions, call (800) 2-IRVING.

HYATT HILL COUNTRY RESORT

Recommended for: golfing, Texas atmosphere, dining

You start your day with a cup of coffee enjoyed in a rocker on a wide porch. Inside the ranch house, some guests sit around an open-hearth stone fireplace, while others take advantage of a lazy morning and sleep late in pine beds beneath quilted comforters.

This may sound like a scene on a Hill Country ranch, but it takes place at the Hyatt Hill Country Resort (9800 Hyatt Resort Dr., 800-233-1234; $$$, ☐) northwest of San Antonio. Built at a cost of $100 million, the 500-room, 200-acre complex is the first Hyatt destination resort in Texas.

Like no other Hyatt, this resort is pure Texas—and with good reason. The resort is located on the former **Rogers-Wiseman Ranch,** a 2,700-acre spread that was family operated for more than a century. Dotted with majestic live oaks and sprinkled with limestone and stands of prickly pear cactus, the ranch rolls across the Hill Country, Texas's richest vacation region. Formed in less time than it takes to describe it, the area was shaped 30 million years ago by a violent 3-1/2-minute earthquake. The convulsion buckled the land north and west of San Antonio, kicking up strata of limestone and granite into rugged hills and steep cliffs.

The jagged scar of the event, the **Balcones Escarpment,** zigzags down the state, marking the frontier between flat farmland toward the east and the rugged ranches to the west. Cotton and cornfields are replaced by hillsides dotted with limestone scrabble, textured by juniper and majestic live oaks, and tinted year-round with wildflowers. The resort took these Hill Country features and incorporated them into the design of the property. The low-rise hotel is divided into nine wings, with views of the ranch at nearly every turn.

The expansive lobby has been constructed to resemble a grand ranchhouse, complete with a wall-sized open fireplace, cowhide chairs, and overstuffed sofas. The ranch look continues in the guest rooms. "We wanted to bring out the craftsmanship of the region—stenciling on the walls, ironwork accessories, and washed-pine-finish beds with tall, carved headboards, footboards, and side rails," explains Connie Jackson, project manager for the hotel's interior designer. "The colors are drawn from those typically found in Hill Country landscape—the blue in blue-bonnets and the red of Indian paintbrush, for example." Details down to mirrors on the bathroom doors, a common feature in Hill Country homes, ring true.

But relaxation just begins in the plush guest rooms—it continues outdoors where couples will find many activities to enjoy year-round. The **Hill Country Golf Club,** an 18-hole championship course, is one of the resort's most popular features. The clubhouse is home to **Antler's Lodge,** a restaurant featuring Southwest cuisine. Lighter fare is offered at the **Cactus Oak Tavern,** located halfway through the course. The **Springhouse Cafe** provides breakfast, lunch, and dinner, including buffet selections.

Water sports are a major activity in the Hill Country and at the resort as well. Grab a tube and jump in the 950-foot-long **Ramblin' River** (heated in cooler months) for a leisurely float around the property. On summer days, enjoy an early morning or late evening float for the quietest ride. When you're finished, head to the adult's-only pool and hot tub, complete with a limestone waterfall.

F Y I

Getting There: The resort is located 20 miles from downtown San Antonio off Loop 1604.

Nearby Attractions: Near the resort lie San Antonio's two theme parks: Sea World of Texas and Fiesta Texas. Fiesta Texas operates in a former limestone quarry. The white, chalky stone used to build homes throughout Central and South Texas was mined from this and similar sites, leaving behind tall limestone cliffs that make dramatic backdrops for the park. Fiesta Texas showcases music, from '50s rock 'n' roll and local *Tejano* sounds to oompah German tunes. The award-winning shows are interspersed with thrill rides, sure to bring a squeal to even the most jaded amusement park goers. Fiesta Texas is open seasonally March through November, with a limited schedule except during summer months. For more information, call (800) 473-4378.

Sea World of Texas, the largest in the Sea World chain, is a marine park that offers equal emphasis on education and fun. Displays and shows featuring orcas, dolphins, seals, and otters partner with an enjoyable water park. Sea World of Texas is open seasonally from March through October, with a limited schedule except during summer months. For more information, call (210) 523-3611.

Children's Program: If you've brought the kids along but you'd still enjoy a romantic getaway, check out Camp Hyatt. This fully supervised program provides fun for young guests 3 to 12 years old. While the little ones enjoy arts and crafts, water sports, and outings, the two of you can take in a game of tennis or golf, a luxurious massage, or just some time alone. Camp Hyatt also offers supervised lunches and dinners. For more information, contact the Recreation Department at (210) 647-1234.

For More Information: For more on the Hyatt Hill Country Resort, call (800) 233-1234. For more on San Antonio attractions, call (800) 447-3372.

LAKE AUSTIN SPA RESORT
Recommended for: relaxation, light dining, exercise together

Lake Austin Spa Resort (1705 Quinlan Pk. Rd., 800-847-5637; $$$, □) proves one thing: that just because something's good for you doesn't mean you won't like it. Sure, your mom once chanted, "Eat it, it's good for you" over a plate of tasteless vegetables, but then your mom wasn't Terry Conlan.

The chief chef of this lakeside resort cooks up a lean, mean menu, one that combines the flavors of the Southwest with healthy ingredients. The author of *Lean Star Cuisine,* Conlan's creations include Enchiladas Verdes, Shrimp Quesadillas with Mango Salsa, Pumpkin Flan, Chocolate Kahlúa Mousse, Crab Cakes with Chipotle Mayonnaise, and more.

Dining at Lake Austin Spa is reason enough to visit, but plenty of other activities await guests. Perched on a quiet shore of Lake Austin in the rolling hills, the resort combines the relaxed charm of a lakeside camp with the luxuries of a health spa to create a casually elegant inn. You'll find plenty of activity here in the form of aerobics classes on a suspended wood floor, tennis, dancing, mountain biking, and even sculling on the lake's calm waters. Activity goes hand-in-hand with relaxation, and here that means stress reduction sessions. For the ultimate in relaxation, enjoy a massage, facial, manicure, aloe vera body masque, invigorating sea salt scrub, or aromatherapy scalp conditioning.

Personal beauty is not the only consideration at the spa—it extends to the setting as well. With a view of a rugged cliff and the sea green waters of **Lake Austin,** the grounds here are as wild as the surrounding Hill Country and populated by wildlife and wildflowers. The beauty continues in the spa buildings. **The Treehouse,** a 4,000-square-foot facility that includes the aerobics studio and a yoga room, is built on pylons that also provide support for a free-flight aviary containing white doves and hummingbirds. Nearby, a limestone waterfall completes the tranquil garden.

Over 40 guest rooms decorated with Shaker-style furnishings are housed in small cottages across the grounds.

F Y I ❧

Getting There: Austin Spa Resort is located off RR 620 northwest of Austin.

For More Information: Call for both day rates and package programs that include three meals daily, fitness activities, and programs. For information, call (800) 847-5637.

ADVENTURES
FOR TWO

GRAB YOUR HIKING BOOTS, SLAP ON SOME sunscreen, and get ready to see the natural side of Texas. Throughout the Lone Star State you can enjoy hiking, camping, caving, and other outdoor activities. The level of difficulty depends on your own abilities. For example, near Fredericksburg you can take a gentle hike up Enchanted Rock where the only required equipment is good walking shoes. Or you can grab your ropes and take off for a climb up the steeper slopes.

Water activities abound in Texas; there are so many, in fact, that we've looked at them in a separate section: "Water Fun."

HILL COUNTRY CAVES
Recommended for: outdoor lovers, spelunking, hot weather getaways

At **Longhorn Caverns State Park** (Park Rd., 4 miles off TX 29, 512-756-4680; admission fee), near Burnet in the Hill Country, you'll hear a story that's the stuff of romance novels.

A century ago, Comanches kidnapped a young woman named Mariel King and brought her back to the cavern. The Indians did not realize they were followed by three Texas Rangers. When the Indians prepared a campfire, the Rangers fired upon them, grabbed Mariel King, and raced for the entrance. Meanwhile, the surviving Comanches regrouped and began their counterattack, falling upon the Rangers before they reached the cavern entrance. A desperate hand-to-hand battle took place, with the Rangers finally escaping with Mariel King. Ending the story with a fairy-tale flourish, Miss King later married one of her rescuers, Logan Van Deveer, and the couple made their home in Burnet.

The cave's other uses weren't quite so romantic. Years later, Confederate soldiers used the cave's main room as a munitions factory. Bat guano from the cave was an ingredient in the manufacture of gunpowder. Additional small rooms in the back reaches of the cavern were used as storerooms for the gunpowder.

The cave went unused for several decades until the Gay Twenties. A local businessman opened a dance hall in the largest room of the cave, building a wooden dance floor several feet above the limestone. When it proved successful, he then opened a restaurant in the next room, lowering food through a hole in the cavern ceiling. Next, an area minister decided to take advantage of the cool temperature and built bleachers to accommodate crowds for Sunday services. When the Depression struck, the cavern was purchased by the state and opened as a park in 1932.

Longhorn Caverns is just one of seven commercial caves in Texas, each offering well-lighted, easy-to-follow trails. Here you'll view a quiet world where progress takes place one drop of water at a time, in a romantic atmosphere cooled by nature's air-conditioning.

The small town of Boerne, northwest of San Antonio on I-10, is home to **Cave Without a Name** (TX 474 north 8 miles from Boerne to Kreutzberg Rd. for 5 miles, 210-537-4212; admission fee). This 50-million-year-old cave is privately owned and, while not as well known as other Hill Country caverns, boasts many beautiful formations. A 45-minute tour takes you through a series of rooms, including one with Texas-sized stalagmites. Gravel walkways wind through the cavern, and the trails are easy to follow.

Nearby **Cascade Caverns** (I-10, exit 543, 210-755-8080; admission fee) is named for its 90-foot waterfall. Cascade Caverns has welcomed the public since 1932, but it's clear that both man and animals have been using the cave much longer. One of the first visitors over 50,000 years ago was a mastodon whose bones remain here today. Later, ancient Indian tribes held ceremonies within the cave's first room, fearing to venture beyond the reassuring sunlight.

The largest cave in the area is **Natural Bridge Caverns** (RR 3009 southwest of New Braunfels, 210-651-6101; admission fee), reminiscent of New Mexico's Carlsbad Caverns. Tours take visitors through enormous rooms that look like the playing fields of prehistoric dinosaurs, rooms with names like "The Castle of the White Giants." Imagine the surprise of four spelunkers from St. Mary's University when they discovered these gargantuan limestone halls in 1960. After their discovery, cave developers worked to carve passages from room to room, resulting in a comfortable walk through this long cavern.

Natural Bridge Caverns takes its name from a rock bridge between two sinkholes, the original entrance to the mouth of the cave. Modern man has known of the sinkholes since the 19th century, but there is evidence of much earlier visitors. Bones of a grizzly bear at least 8,000 years old have been discovered, as well as human bones, stone weapons, and other Indian artifacts.

North of San Antonio on I-35 is **Wonder Cave** (Wonder World Dr. exit off I-35 S., 512-392-3760; admission fee), a cavern where you won't see sparkling formations, waterfalls, or auditorium-sized rooms. What you will see is a very unique attraction: a view of the Balcones Fault from inside the fault. The cave was produced during a 3-1/2-minute earthquake 30 million years ago, the same one that formed the Balcones Fault, an 1,800-mile line separating the western Hill Country from the flat eastern farmland. Within the cave, you'll see boulders lodged in the fissure. Wonder Cave is open from March until November.

Continue north on I-35 to Georgetown, home of **Inner Space** (I-35 exit 259, 512-863-5545; admission fee). The cave was discovered in 1963 when road crews building the highway drilled into one of the large rooms. Consequent drilling and exploration revealed that a major cavern wound below the proposed highway. Remains of Ice Age mastodons, wolves, sabre-toothed tigers, and a glyptodon (a kind of pre-historic armadillo) have been discovered here, and an 80-foot cavern wall has been decorated with a modern artist's renderings of these ancient creatures.

Finally, the **Caverns of Sonora** (I-10 west of Junction to RM 1989, 915-387-3105; admission fee) have been described by some cave experts as the most beautiful in the world. This scenic spot offers two tours, a 45-minute and a 75-minute version, presenting visitors with spectacular stalactites and stalagmites as well as unusual butterfly-shaped formations.

FOSSIL RIM WILDLIFE CENTER
Recommended for: animal lovers, eco-tourists

It's the dream of many couples: to one day leave their jobs, travel around the world, and eventually find a job that becomes a passion they both can share. That's exactly what happened to husband-wife team Jim Jackson and Christine Jurzykowski. Jackson is a for-mer decorated U.S. Army helicopter pilot and custom woodworker who is still presi-dent of the couple's sailboat-building com-pany, Deerfoot Yachts. Jurzykowski is a former film producer whose New York film company produced everything from commercials to fea-ture films (including *The Handmaid's Tale*).

"In 1983 we both decided that life was too short to continue what we were doing," recalls Jurzykowski. "We moved onto a sailboat and had visions of sailing around the world. We saw a documentary, and it started us on a long journey, and we started hatching out some plans."

Those plans eventually led the couple to Glen Rose, southwest of Fort Worth, and to the ranch that would become Fossil Rim Wildlife Center (US 67, 3 miles west of Glen Rose, 817-897-4967 or 897-2960;

admission fee), a 3,000-acre privately owned conservation center. Something about the rugged landscape of the Texas Hill Country struck a resonating chord. "We really felt that it was meant to be and that we were supposed to be here."

What this couple has created is a unique park where, for a few days, guests live among 1,000 animals representing 30 endangered and exotic species. Visitors enjoy air-conditioned and centrally heated tent cabins, gourmet meals, and all the joys of a safari without any of the hassles.

"Imagine yourself going to Africa without the plane ride, the shots, or the worries," says Christine Jurzykowski, co-owner of Fossil Rim. "There are two main differences between what you experience in Africa and what you'll see here. Here you will see more animals in a shorter time, and here you will not see something like a cheetah killing a gazelle. Otherwise, in terms of behavior, you will witness things here you would see in Africa, but you will do it in extreme luxury."

Texas is dotted with drive-through animal parks, but Fossil Rim is in a class by itself, combining entertainment with education and scientific research. "It's been a roller-coaster ride with lots of lessons and journeys," recalls Jurzykowski. "As we've learned, it has been a plus that we weren't trained. We were able to bring a different perspective. Fossil Rim has moved to bring new resources into conservation." Today the center employs as many as 80 people, whose jobs range from construction to education to research. Visiting scientists from around the world conduct internships at the center.

The couple has created a living laboratory focused on endangered species, but with the general public in mind as well. Visitors can enjoy Fossil Rim for a day or several days. Accommodations include tent camping and group cabins, but most popular is the **safari program.** Safaris are booked for groups only; contact Fossil Rim or Texas Passport Adventures (see Appendix). Visitors are picked up at the **Welcoming Center** in an open-air safari vehicle and whisked to safari camp out in the Texas ranchland. Similarities to the African savanna make many of the animals feel right at home and make guests feel they've traveled to the Dark Continent to observe and learn about wildlife such as the cheetah, giraffe, wildebeest, and rhino.

On these three- or four-day excursions, safari participants enjoy game drives in open vehicles led by naturalists who point out and identify the animals roaming free on the ranch. Guests can go behind the scenes to talk to veterinarians who care for and study these exotic species about which little is known. There are also nature walks, bird watches, horseback rides, hikes, and expeditions to study 66-million-year-old fossils on the ranch. Once an inland sea, this region is rich with fossils. In more recent times the Comanches camped here, adding their own artifacts to Fossil Rim's archaeological heritage.

One of the most exciting activities at Fossil Rim is a trip to the **Intensive Management Area,** a part of the ranch open only to safari visitors and those who take part in behind-the-scene tours. The IMA houses special residents such as red wolves, long-legged maned wolves from South America, cheetahs, black rhinos, and Attwater's prairie chickens. Although it might seem that the cheetah and the Attwater's prairie chicken, a native of the Texas coastal plains, have little in common, they share a sad fate—both risk extinction without the efforts of agencies like Fossil Rim. This facility has the first of only three captive populations of the Attwater's prairie chickens in the world (less than 500 are living in the wild). When settlers first crossed the coastal plains to settle the West, these birds numbered over a million.

Fossil Rim's **cheetah breeding program** has been highly successful, so much so that now approximately 20 percent of all cheetahs in the U.S. trace their lineage back to the Center. The cheetahs are housed in a long, narrow containment, permitting them to race around their enclosure at the blinding speeds they would clock in the wild. In addition to the breeding program, Fossil Rim also conducts several research projects aimed at increasing the cheetah's chances of survival. In one such project, Fossil Rim, along with Washington, D.C.'s, National Zoo, is studying the cheetah's reproductive physiology. From this project came the first surviving litters of cheetahs conceived through artificial insemination. The cubs were born in 1992.

After a day of safari activities, guests head back to camp for cocktails and an elegant dinner of Rock Cornish game hen or tenderloin of pork. After dinner, everyone gathers on the deck to enjoy a campfire and swap stories about the day's safari. Visitors also can continue their nature viewing, albeit thousands of miles away, through powerful telescopes aimed at the heavens.

Finally, Fossil Rim also welcomes **day visitors** to enjoy a nine-mile drive through the ranch, feeding animals along the way. This drive winds through four areas, each containing free-roaming animal populations moving in herds. You'll probably see sable antelope, Grevy's zebra, oryx, and greater kudu, as well as gazelle and ostrich. The highlight for many is a chance to feed the reticulated giraffes—shy, silent giants that tower nearly as high as the oak trees.

Halfway through the drive, guests can stop at **The Overlook** for a chance to stroke a pot-bellied pig at the petting farm, shop in the nature store, grab a burger at the snack bar, or stretch their legs on a short nature walk. The best attraction at The Overlook is, as the name suggests, the panoramic view. Here, from atop the fossil-encrusted rim for which the ranch is named, guests can see across the valleys and surrounding hills. For exotic animals thousands of miles from their native lands, this Texas ranch is more than just a new home. By providing protection from the forces that have brought them near extinction, Fossil Rim offers endangered species something more: hope.

It's that hope that motivates the research at Fossil Rim and sets the standard for a program with global proportions. Countries including Guatemala and Costa Rica have asked Fossil Rim to bring its conservation program to their countries. It's a plan that focuses not only on the animals but on the human residents of the regions as well.

"We take an integrated approach to the issues and challenges of conservation. You cannot just look at the habitat but also the problems of people and the economy. We combine science and humanism to deal with some of the problems," says Jurzykowski.

Jurzykowski and Jackson refer to Fossil Rim as a living experiment, a place where knowledge can be obtained and species continued so that, as world conditions stabilize, they can be reintroduced into the wild. "Our ultimate mission is for Fossil Rim to go extinct," explains Jurzykowski, looking over a prairie dotted with species she hopes will one day be again roaming the wild. "At that point, Fossil Rim would not be necessary."

F Y I 〰

Getting There: Glen Rose is an hour southwest of Fort Worth or two hours northeast of Waco on US 67. Fossil Rim is located about three miles west of town.

Nearby Attractions: Save time for a stop by Dinosaur Valley State Park (4 miles north of Glen Rose on Park Rd. 59, 817-897-4588; admission fee). Situated along the Paluxy River, this park is known for its dinosaur tracks. You'll find the tracks in the river bed, so bring hiking and wading shoes. Six miles of hiking trails invite couples to explore the park. Campsites and picnic tables are also available.

Festivals/Special Events: Throughout the year, Fossil Rim hosts special tours, including the Wolf Howl, the Owl Prowl, and, for romantics, a moonlight safari. The "Candlelight and Moonlight Safari" starts with drinks and hors d'oeuvres and continues with an elegant meal such as stuffed artichokes with red pepper vinaigrette, marinated chicken bedded on red Bibb lettuce, and garlic-rosemary shrimp kabobs.

Love Nests: If you'd rather stay in town, check out the Inn on the River (205 S.W. Barnard St., 817-897-2101; $$$, ☐). This adults-only property is located on the banks of the Paluxy River in downtown Glen Rose. Built in 1919, the hotel has 19 rooms and three suites, each with a private bath. Weekend guests can enjoy four-course gourmet dinners as well.

For More Information: For more information on Fossil Rim Wildlife Center, call (817) 897-4967. For a packet of brochures on the Glen Rose area, call the Glen Rose Chamber of Commerce at (817) 897-2286.

ENCHANTED ROCK
Recommended for: hikes, picnics camping

Imagine a hike in the moonlight on a bald stone mountain. Against the rugged pink granite, an occasional moonbeam catches a shallow puddle, reflecting a star-speckled sky. In the distance, mile after mile of Hill Country landscape lies illuminated, the rolling hills broken up only by an occasional ranch house.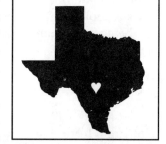

This is **Enchanted Rock State Park** (18 miles north of Fredericksburg on RR 965, 915-247-3903; admission fee), site of Texas's most romantic moonlit walk. But if sunlight is more your thing, you'll also find that this park is filled with opportunities for hiking, picnicking, and primitive camping.

Enchanted Rock looms over the Texas hillside like a massive bald mountain, an enormous dome of pink granite that rises 325 feet above the small stream flowing at its base. Covering over a square mile, the formation is second in size only to Georgia's Stone Mountain. Over the years, rumors about the rock have been plentiful: it glows in the dark, human sacrifices were held on its smooth granite surface, it moans at night, it hides veins of gold and diamonds, it is haunted. Everything about this rock, from the name to the legends, is enchanted.

Located north of Fredericksburg in the heart of the Hill Country, the land here is covered with live oaks, sharp rock formations, and steep hills that jut from the land. No other outcroppings in the area compare to this granite monolith, though, which catches the attention of travelers even miles away. Today the park is a favorite playground for rock climbers, backpackers, and even sedentary tourists who don't mind a lung-expanding walk up the dome for a look at mile after mile of rural Texas.

The history behind the formation of Enchanted Rock dates back over a billion years ago when the earth was in a great upheaval. Moving underground masses produced the rock. When it was first formed, the giant creation was covered by dirt. The actual face of the rock appeared on the scene about 600 million years ago, when erosion removed all the sediment and left the bald mountain exposed.

Over the years, the stone has been heated and cooled so many times that giant cracks run through the surface, giving the appearance of great sheets of rock that seem ready to flake off and slide down the mountain. This heating and cooling process continues every day, and it's said to account for the noises that come from the rock in the dark, cool hours of the night—though area Indians believed that those creaking sounds came from a less worldly source. A legend told of a young Indian woman who was brought to the apex of the stone by her father, an ambitious chieftain. Eager to win the favor of his gods, he sacrificed his daughter. Too late he learned that the offering was condemned. As punishment, the gods commanded his unhappy spirit to wander forever the surface of Enchanted Rock.

Not all the tales of Enchanted Rock are fiction, however. Near the summit, a bronze plaque recounts the escape of Texas Ranger Captain Jack Hays from the Comaches in 1841. Surprised and cut off from his companions, Hays fled up the rock and hid in one of the cracks that cover its surface, pursued by angry Comanches who were convinced that Hays had violated the sanctity of their sacred mountain. The Ranger managed to avoid capture and, thanks to his superior weapons, killed so many Comanches that the rest quickly abandoned the chase when Hays's companions arrived on the scene.

Today the face of Enchanted Rock is little changed from those pioneer days. Although at first look the granite appears to be barren of any plant life, scattered shallow pools of rainwater grow wild onion and lichen. Several small trees grow near the summit, and wildlife also thrives on the rock. The collared lizard, a green, yellow, and red iguana cousin with a black and white collar, calls Enchanted Rock home. Many species of birds circle the rock, and most days you'll be able to see buzzards, miles away, hovering over a potential meal. Keep an eye out for mockingbirds as well as hawks, doves, and bobwhites.

The entire park is of interest to biologists, botanists, and geologists, who now know that Enchanted Rock is composed of granite. Years ago, however, speculators had different ideas about the rock—the promise of precious metals and gems lured the earliest Europeans to the vicinity. The Spanish began organizing explorations of the area in 1753 after hearing reports of "a red mountain." Small samples of silver-bearing ore were sent back to San Antonio for analysis, but the silver was of inferior quality. Rumors of vast gold and silver treasures hoarded by the Indians continued to attract the Spaniards' attention, though. By the time settlers from the U.S. arrived in Texas, the folklore concerning Enchanted Rock dictated that the entire rock was a giant gold nugget. Later, Texas pioneer Stephen F. Austin said that the hill was pure iron.

See the granite for yourself with a walk up the dome. Bring your best walking shoes for the trek. Except when wet or icy, it's a fairly easy climb, and the view is worth the effort. Experienced climbers can scale the smaller formations located adjacent to the main dome. These bare rocks are steep and dotted with boulders and crevices, and their ascent requires special equipment.

F Y I ◈

Getting There: To reach the park, drive west from Austin on US 290. In Fredericksburg, turn north on RM 965. Don't worry, there's no way to miss it—it's the first pink mountain on the left.

Love Nests: Enchanted Rock lies in prime B&B territory. For details, see "Fredericksburg" in the "Bed-and-Breakfast Getaways" chapter of this book. If you'd like to extend your stay within the park, tent camping and primitive backpack camping is available.

For More Information: For more information on Enchanted Rock State Park, call (915) 247-3903. Admission is limited on busy weekends, so schedule a weekday visit if possible.

ROCKPORT
Recommended for: bird watching, beach fun

"There's a buff-belly at the feeder!" Within seconds, the tiny hummingbird is under careful scrutiny by 30 pairs of eyes, all aided by high-powered binoculars and zoom lenses. Field guides appear from a number of pockets as the birders seek to confirm the sighting. Soon smiles break out among the crowd—this was a buff-bellied, after all. The trip to Rockport, which some of the group had made from surrounding states, was a success.

This scene is repeated time and time again during the fall hummingbird migration through the Coastal Bend and particularly Rockport. During August and September, thousands of tiny hummers from as far as Canada use this coastal community as a filling station, a place to stop and refuel before the arduous, nonstop journey over the Gulf on their way to warmer climes in Mexico and Central and South America. Along with the clouds of tiny birds come flocks of birders. Binoculars in hand, they migrate to Rockport in pursuit of several hummingbird species, hoping to add another name to their life list of identified birds.

The Rockport-Fulton area has long been known as a birders' paradise. Connie Hagar, amateur ornithologist and a legend in this coastal village, focused the eyes (and binoculars) of the birdwatching community on the Coastal Bend. She moved to Rockport in 1935 and for 3-1/2 decades chronicled the comings and goings of hundreds of species. Ever since, birders have flocked to Rockport for a look at everything from whooping cranes to painted buntings.

During the fall migration, they come to see the hummingbirds, an annual pilgrimage that has become a festival—the **Hummer/Bird Celebration.** The Coastal Bend Audubon Society together with the neighboring communities of Rockport and Fulton have come together to host the celebration. At the festival, you can attend workshops such as "Birding for Beginners," "Shorebird Identification," and "Creating Backyard Habitats." To help with bird identification and to provide some background on the migrating species, videotape presentations run nonstop at the center. Booths sell everything from hummingbird feeders to T-shirts featuring the tiny guests.

But the high points of the festival are the Audubon-guided bus tours with stops at private homes and fishing camps in Bayside and surrounding communities, some sites with 10 or more feeders. Buzzing like huge bees, the hummers congregate in swarms of as many as 100 to 200 birds. Because they are concentrating on feeding, you are able to walk very near. The hungry hummers are not afraid of a quiet, slow-moving audience.

The bus tours also stop at other birding sites on the coastal grasslands for a look at other migratory species. Your guide will identify birds, furnish background information on the birds you are watching, and set up high-powered viewing scopes. Rockport has over 500 species on record, including a large number of shorebirds.

Although the Hummer/Bird Celebration recognizes all of Rockport's feathered friends, it's the tiny hummer who steals the show. In recent years the city has made a concerted effort to attract the hummers, sponsoring workshops and classes for would-be hosts. As a result, citizens have planted bushes and vines to attract the migrators to backyard habitats.

The hummers are fast-moving, but because of the large number in Rockport during migration, they're easy to spot. Rockport is located on the Central Flyway, a bird highway that brings migrators from Canada, through Montana, and over the Central states on their way to Mexico. Rockport also receives a few strays from the Mississippi Flyway, a combination that makes the area a hummer hotspot.

Even if you can't make it to Rockport for the Hummer/Bird Celebration, you're heading into a birding paradise no matter what the season. Winter and spring offer prime viewing months, with up to 200 species a day spotted during spring migration. The winter brings many birders to the area for a look at the magnificent whooping crane, a bird that stands five feet tall and winters in the marshy lands near the Aransas National Wildlife Refuge.

The **Aransas National Wildlife Refuge** (45 min. northeast of Rockport via Hwy. 35, 512-286-3559; admission fee) is a protected area known primarily for the whooping cranes. The Visitors Center features mounted specimens of whoopers from egg to adulthood, along with films on the birds' behavior and migration. Across from the Visitors Center you'll find an alligator pond with plenty of toothy specimens, and several nearby hiking trails invite you to take a (careful) walk in the wildlife-filled area. The refuge is also home to shrew, armadillo, coyote, jackrabbit, red wolf, gray fox, ringtail, raccoon, coati, mink, weasel, badger, wild boar, peccary, deer, mountain lion, and bobcat. Don't be surprised to see dolphins in the waters of the refuge, and all along the Gulf coast and bays. The playful mammals are a common sight, especially near boats.

The refuge also has a whooping crane viewing platform, but you'll still be some distance from the birds. The best look awaits aboard one of the whooping crane tours, the cream of which is Captain Ted's Whooping Crane Tour, operating from November through March. Aboard the **M. V. Skimmer** (800-338-4551; admission fee), specially designed for the very shallow waters of the bay, you'll cruise within yards of the whooping crane families. If you're too late for the whoopers, you can take a rookery tour aboard the *Skimmer* from April through June to see the largest reddish egret rookery in the world.

Of course, this coastal community is more than a birding hotspot—it's a romantic hotspot as well. Walk on the sands at **Rockport Beach Park** (off TX 35; admission fee) along more than a mile of beach and shop for local artwork at the **Rockport Center for the Arts** (Navigation Circle, in town, 512-729-5519; free). Just down the street from the Art Center, you'll find the **Texas Maritime Museum** (1202 Navigation Circle, 512-729-5519; admission fee), which covers maritime history from the Spanish shipwrecks off the Gulf coast to the offshore oil industry. You'll find exhibits on shipbuilding, small boat building, and "Texans of the Sea."

When you visit Rockport, you're entering an area that helped Texas become the number one birding destination in the world. Rockport is more than happy to admit that this place is "for the birds!"

F Y I

Getting There: Rockport is located 31 miles northeast of Corpus Christi on Highway 35.

Festivals/Special Events: Rockport is a festive city, and it shows. Besides the Hummer/Bird Celebration, you'll find festivals year-round. Rockport Seafair is held the weekend before Columbus Day, the Mexican-themed Fiesta En La Playa is celebrated every Labor Day weekend, the Rockport Art Festival marks the Fourth of July weekend, and the Fulton Oysterfest livens up the first weekend of March. During the winter months, special events are planned regularly for the many RV residents, including fishing and horseshoe tournaments, and several arts and crafts shows.

Dining: The *Skimmer* is docked next to the Sanddollar Restaurant (109 N. Fulton Rd., 512-729-8909; $$, ☐), one of Rockport's many excellent seafood establishments. This waterfront restaurant boasts a wonderful view of the Aransas Bay and serves seafood so fresh they swear it slept in the sea the night before! You'll also find fresh Gulf shrimp at one of our favorite restaurants in the state: the Boiling Pot (Fulton Beach Rd., 512-729-6972; $$, ☐), a rollicking place with spicy Cajun shrimp and crab served on your tablecloth of white butcher paper. It's a roll-up-your-sleeves kind of place that's always busy.

Love Nests: Rockport has a huge selection of accommodations, ranging from fishing cottages to elegantly furnished condominiums. Because of the large number of Winter Texans who call Rockport home during the cooler months up North, there are many RV and trailer parks and condominiums that lease by the day, week, or month. For a brochure listing all of Rockport-Fulton's varied lodgings, call the Chamber of Commerce office at (800) 242-0071 or (800) 826-6441.

One of our favorite places to stay is Key Allegro (1798 Bayshore Dr., just over Key Allegro Bridge on Fulton Beach Rd., 512-729-2333 or 800-348-1627; $–$$$, ☐). This small island is linked to Rockport by an arched bridge. The lovely drive here is your first hint at the elegant accommodations awaiting visitors in this area. Nicely appointed condominium units and upscale homes located on the water's edge afford beautiful views of Rockport's fishing vessels heading out for the day's catch. Rental homes and condominiums are available by the day or week.

For B&B accommodations, check out The Blue Heron Inn (801 Patton St., 512-729-7526; $, ☐). Overlooking Little Bay, the inn features four guest rooms decorated with local artwork. Another popular B&B is Anthony's by the Sea (732 S. Pearl St., 800-460-2557; $, ☐). This inn includes a honeymoon suite and guest houses equipped with a full kitchen. In neighboring Fulton, The Rodmaker's House (5030 N. Hwy. 35, 512-790-8145; $, ☐) will be popular with fishermen; owner Dennis Freeman is considered one of the top custom rodmakers in the state.

Bridal Bits: For romantic elegance that captures the spirit of the Victorian era, consider an outdoor wedding on the grounds of the Fulton Mansion (317 N. Fulton Beach Rd., 512-729-0386). The lush grounds, just steps from Aransas Bay, are dotted with towering palms and majestic oaks.

For More Information: For more on this coastal community, call the Rockport/Fulton Area Chamber of Commerce at (800) 242-0071.

BIG BEND
Recommended for: hiking, rafting, star gazing

Looking for a peek at the way Texas used to be? Then head off to Big Bend, one of the most rugged areas of the state. Formed by a southerly dip in the Rio Grande, this country is often referred to as the Lone Star State's "last frontier." Here the land stretches unbroken by highways or highline wires, all the way to the horizon. It's a region of stark canyons and desert blooms, where sunsets explode nightly across the technicolor sky.

It may be remote, but this area is rich with attractions—both of the natural and man-made varieties. Your first look at the Big Bend region is Fort Stockton, the largest city in the area. Located on I-10, it's the most accessible town in the region. Stop first at the **Visitor Information Caboose** (I-10 and Highway 285, 915-336-8052) for free brochures.

Fort Stockton has several attractions, including the **Annie Riggs Museum** (301 S. Main, 915-336-2167; admission fee). Housed in the 1900 Victorian Hotel, today this adobe structure is filled with local history exhibits. The town is also home to the **Ste. Genevieve Winery** (25 miles east of town). Tours of the winery, the fifth largest in the U.S. and the largest in the state, are available only on Saturday through Roadrunner Bus Tours. For details call the Chamber of Commerce at (800) 336-2166, or stop by the Visitors Information Caboose.

Heading south from Fort Stockton on US 385, near the same route covered by the Comanche War Trial, is the town of Marathon. Historic hotel lovers know Marathon for its **Gage Hotel** built in 1927 (see "Love Nests").

West of Marathon on US 90 lies the picturesque community of Alpine. Perched at an elevation of 4,481 feet, this tree-shaded community enjoys a temperate climate and beautiful vistas. From here you'll see mountain peaks over 6,000 feet in elevation, projections that soar from the floor of the Chihuahuan Desert.

Fort Davis, north on TX 118, is called the "highest town in Texas" at 5,050 feet. Here you can visit **Fort Davis National Historic Site**

(915-426-3224; admission fee), where restored buildings recall the city's founding in 1854 as a U.S. military post.

Lovers can gaze at the stars at the **McDonald Observatory** (TX 118 N. 16 miles to Mt. Locke, 915-426-3640; small admission fee). Internationally known, the observatory is staffed by researchers and offers viewing, observatory tours, and a visitors center that's open daily. The most spectacular views occur during "Star Parties," held on Tuesday, Friday, and Saturday evenings. Here you can take in the heavens over West Texas by means of the telescopes provided. (Bring a jacket even during warm months because the desert air is chilly.)

South of Fort Davis on US Highway 67 lies the community of Marfa, home of Texas's most unusual phenomena. Here, nine miles east of town, folks gather to view the mysterious **Marfa lights.** A historic marker identifies the spot where the lights have been seen for over a century. The viewing area fills with cars nightly as curious onlookers come in hopes of a glimpse of the lights, whose cause has never been explained. Search the horizon for the lights, which are seen year-round but not every night.

South of Marfa lies **Big Bend National Park** (915-477-2291; admission fee). This may be the most rugged area of Texas, but it's a fragile ecosystem. Travel carefully here and realize that the plant life has a tenuous hold in the rocky terrain.

Outdoor activities—from easy walks to strenuous climbs, from camping to photography—abound throughout the park. You'll find that, although roads cover the park, one of the most popular ways to view the area is aboard white-water rafts. Guided float trips (or individual ones with a free park permit) cover the region. You can spend a day or two weeks floating the river in style. Outfitters include **Texas River Expeditions** (800-839-7238), **Big Bend River Tours** (800-542-4240), **Far Flung Adventures** (800-359-4138), and **Outback Expeditions** (800-343-1640).

F Y I ❧

Getting There: Big Bend is not an area you stumble upon as you journey along. To reach this remote region, you must be headed here. To drive to Big Bend, follow I-10 or US 90 to US 385. Turn south and continue to Big Bend National Park. This is not Yellowstone—don't expect guided tour buses to help you with transportation needs. A vehicle is a necessity, so make prior arrangements for rental cars.

Festivals/Special Events: If you're a follower of unexplained phenomena, then head to Marfa for the Marfa Light Festival on Labor Day weekend. The Marfa lights, seen most nights outside the city, have been spotted since 1883 and sometimes appear very bright, other times dim. The three-day celebration includes arts and crafts, food booths, and plenty of discussion about the mysterious lights. For more information, call the Marfa Chamber of Commerce at (915) 729-4942.

In November, the ghost town of Terlingua bubbles with the Frank X. Tolbert/Wick Fowler Memorial Championship Cookoff. Held the first Saturday of November, this is the biggest event in this area. This cook-off is one of the most serious ones in a state that's mighty serious about its chili. During the three-day event, the otherwise quiet town of Terlingua bursts with thousands of cooks and tasters who come to enjoy the chili cook-off as well as a "margarita mix-off," a barbecue cook-off, a bean cook-off, and country music (903-874-5601).

Love Nests: Similarly, you also need to make prior arrangements for accommodations in this remote area. A night spent in the back seat of your car sounds romantic, but you'll be left with painful souvenir and a sure way to kill romance—a sore back and a stiff neck.

One of the best known facilities in this part of the state is the Gage Hotel (Hwy. 90 in Marathon, 800-884-GAGE; $, □). This restored state historical landmark has both old and new sections (in the new section, some rooms include fireplaces).

In the Davis Mountains State Park, make your reservations early for the Indian Lodge (Davis Mountains State Park, 915-426-3254; $, □). Built by the CCC, this 39-room classic inn features rooms with pine and latrilla cane ceilings. The hotel includes a restaurant.

Also in Fort Davis, The Hotel Limpia (Main St. on the Square, 800-662-5517; $, □) offers 32 quiet rooms in a historic inn dating back 80 years.

In Big Bend National Park, the Chisos Mountains Lodge (915-477-2291; $, □) offers 72 motel accommodations and stone cottages at an elevation of 5,400 feet above sea level.

For More Information: For Fort Davis information, call the Chamber of Commerce at (800) 524-3015 or write Box 378, Fort Davis, TX 79734. For Marfa, call the Marfa Chamber of Commerce at (915) 729-4942. For more on the park contact the Superintendent, Big Bend National Park, TX 79834, or call (915) 477-2251.

WATER FUN

ASK ANY TEXAN WHAT'S THE BEST SUMMER getaway, and he'll tell you anyplace close to water. When temperatures soar higher than a Houston skyscraper, couples look for trips that offer a chance to splash in some of the state's best swimming holes.

For retreats along the Gulf coast, check out the "Coastal Getaways" chapter.

HIGHLAND LAKES

Recommended for: birdwatching, sunset watching, winery, lake cruise

Slowly the boat winds its way up the wide river, passing a pair of white-tailed deer along the banks. A great blue heron fishes the tree-lined shallows on long graceful legs. A steep bluff dotted with yucca and prickly pear casts its shadow on the waters below.

This may sound like a scene from Texas's past, but it greets boaters daily at Lake Buchanan. Aboard the **Vanishing Texas River Cruise** (RM 2341, follow signs, 512-756-6986; admission fee), you have the chance to look at a slice of Texas removed from harried highways and bustling business. Kick off your shoes, settle back in a deck chair, and watch a little bit of Texas drift by while someone else takes over the driving.

The Vanishing Texas River Cruise originates about 50 miles northwest of Austin on **Lake Buchanan,** the largest in the Highland Lakes chain. Although you probably think of boating as a summer activity, this cruise is perhaps best known as a wintertime treat. That's because these cold-weather cruises feature a sight that's found in Texas only during the winter—the American bald eagle. Aboard one of the multilevel cruise boats, winter visitors can float through eagle country for a rare look at our national bird, all from within the confines of the glass-enclosed decks or, for real bird-lovers, from the open-air top deck.

The eagles are popular with birdwatching groups and photographers, but other birds seen along the cruise route have their share of fans also. Egrets, blue herons, a variety of ducks, kingfishers, wild turkey, white pelicans, and sea gulls are seen regularly at various times of the year. Some, such as the gulls and the pelicans, follow the tour boats closely, looking for handouts.

But with warmer weather and the departure of the eagles, you'll find many other attractions along the rugged shoreline. In the spring, wildflowers are popular sights. Bluebonnets, red Indian paintbrushes, and multicolored firewheels turn the riverbanks into colorful tapestries during the months of April and May.

During the summer, voyagers can spot deer, feral hogs, and wild turkey as they come from the hills to drink at the river's edge. And warm summer evenings are perfect for sitting on the top deck and taking life easy.

The cruise also passes by the fields of **Falls Creek Vineyards** (2.2 miles northeast of Tow Post Office on FM 2241, 915-379-5361; free). Save time after your cruise to return to the winery for a tour and taste of their award-winning product.

For a look at other lakes along the Highland Lakes chain, created in 1937, drive south from Lake Buchanan. Inks Lake, the second in the chain, is a small lake only three miles long, but it has a special charm all its own. Much of the water's edge is lined with homes, and a large section is bordered by the **Inks Lake State Park** (Park Rd. 4 off TX 29, 512-793-2223; admission fee). This 1,200-acre park is the largest of any of the Highland Lakes parks, with a 143 campsites, fishing piers, a concession for buying groceries or bait, and a nine-hole golf course. Nearby lies Longhorn Caverns (see the "Adventures for Two" chapter).

Travel down FM 1431 to the third in the lake chain, **Lake LBJ.** Renamed for Texas's hometown boy, Lyndon Baines Johnson, the lake is protected by tall granite cliffs which shield it from gusty winds. Because of the calm waters, skiers and fishermen are attracted in droves.

Next is **Lake Marble Falls,** named for the slick marble ledges that formed a waterfall and a natural lake. Today these falls are hidden in the depths beneath Lake Marble Falls and seen only when the water level drops.

You may not get to view the marble falls, but there's no way to miss the granite for which Marble Falls is famous. This glimmering stone is everywhere, from the bluffs lining the lake to the picnic areas at City Park. In fact, one of the largest quarry operations of its kind is found on Granite Mountain, just west of the town of Marble Falls. Pink granite from the quarry was used to construct the nation's largest state capitol building in Austin, Texas. A century ago, hundreds of stonecutters from Scotland along with gangs of Texas convicts performed the back-breaking work of cutting the stone from Granite Mountain.

The rough, rocky terrain of Marble Falls diminishes somewhat by the time you reach **Lake Travis,** a large, meandering lake that winds its way from the Hill Country to Austin's front door. At 65 miles long, Travis is the longest lake in the chain and over three miles across in some spots, with literally hundreds of coves and inlets along its snake-like boundaries. Much of the land on Travis's shores is controlled by the LCRA and remains undeveloped, but there are several excellent public parks from which to choose.

For couples looking for something a little different than the usual sunbathing, a popular spot is **McGregor/Hippie Hollow Park** (Comanche Tr. off RR 620, 512-266-1644; admission fee). This is a clothing-optional park, the only one in the Austin area. On summer weekends, it is packed with nudists, curious onlookers, and swimmers who want to enjoy a beautiful swimming hole. Onlookers outnumber nudists many weekends, but to see the beach (and the swimmers) you must leave your car and walk down the trail to the water's edge. The swimming area is protected from curious boaters, who are kept at a distance by patrolling Parks Department boats.

If you're at Lake Travis at sunset, stop by the **Oasis Cantina del Lago** (6550 Comanche Tr., 512-266-2441; $$, □), where Austinites flock to watch an unparalleled sunset from the restaurant's multilevel decks.

When the day draws to a close, the sun bathes the lake in orange and red tones and a quiet comes over the water. As the last of the boats drift in for the night, the Hill Country wildlife move in on the shoreline. Whether it's a raccoon washing his evening meal or a white-tailed deer coming down for a cool drink, the lake returns to its rightful owners. And that's the way the people of the Hill Country—and the couples lucky enough to spend a few days here—hope it will remain.

F Y I ✎

Getting There: The Highland Lakes are located in the heart of the Hill Country, northwest of Austin. From I-35, travel west on FM 1431 to turnoffs for Lake Travis, Lake Marble Falls, Inks Lake, Lake LBJ, and Lake Buchanan. The fastest route to Lake Buchanan is via TX 29, west from I-35 in Georgetown.

Vanishing Texas River Cruise: For information on the cruise, call (512) 756-6986 or write the Vanishing Texas River Cruise at P.O. Box 901, Burnet, TX 78611. Reservations are required. The 2-1/2-hour river cruises launch at 11 a.m., every day of the year except Christmas. Sunset cruises run May through October.

Love Nests: Enjoy what some say is Texas's prettiest sunset at the Oasis Guest Suites (adjacent to the Oasis Cantina del Lago, 512-266-2441; $$$, □). Perched 450 feet over Lake Travis, these multilevel cottages include a fireplace, two baths, a loft, and a pool. No children under 12 are permitted here, and no smoking is allowed inside.

For more traditional hotel accommodations on Lake Travis, try the Lakeway Inn (101 Lakeway Dr., 800-LAKEWAY or 512-261-6600; $$–$$$, □). Located in the golf community of Lakeway on Lake Travis, this large hotel has 170 rooms featuring Southwest decor and a lake view. Some accommodations include fireplaces and kitchens. A lobby bar serves evening cocktails, and an attractive restaurant offers breakfast, lunch, and dinner.

On Lake LBJ, Horseshoe Bay Resort and Conference Club (RR 2147, west of Marble Falls, 800-252-9363 in TX or 800-531-5105 outside TX; $$$; □) is one of the premier resorts in Central Texas. Golfers have their choice of three courses, including Applerock, designed by Robert Trent Jones. Other features include Oriental gardens, a yacht club, horseback trails, and tennis courts.

On Lake Buchanan, check out Buchanan Yacht Resort (TX 261, 512-793-2568; $, □). This comfortable resort is perfect for kicking back and enjoying some fishing, hiking, or just relaxation on the lake shores. While many of the resort buildings are designed for families and groups, the honeymoon cabin is a perfect getaway.

For More Information: Contact the Burnet Chamber of Commerce, Drawer M, Burnet, TX 78611, or call (512) 756-4297. For information on the upper lake chain, contact the Lake Buchanan Chamber of Commerce, P.O. Box 282, Buchanan Dam, TX 78609, or call (512) 793-2803.

SAN MARCOS
Recommended for: river activities, outlet shopping, B&Bs

If you're interested in ecotourism, then sample Texas's natural attributes. San Marcos, located between San Antonio and Austin, is a town filled with attractions that highlight the native features of this riverside area. "San Marcos, A Texas Natural" is more than a slogan—it's a description of what draws visitors to this city of just over 36,000 permanent residents. To many Texans, San Marcos is the  home of the largest collection of outlet stores in the state, but the city's real attractions stretch west of the interstate highway.

Many of these treasures lie along the banks of the San Marcos River, suspected to be the longest continually inhabited site in North America. Used by man for over 13,000 years, it flows through town and provides the city with beautiful swimming and snorkeling spots.

The best known attraction on the river is **Aquarena Springs** (take Aquarena Springs exit off I-35 and follow signs, 800-999-9767 or 512-396-8900; admission fee). This family park dates back to 1928, when A. B. Rogers purchased 125 acres at the headwaters of the San Marcos River to create a grand hotel. He added glass-bottomed boats to cruise Spring Lake, fed by over 200 springs that produce 150 million gallons daily. This 98-percent-pure water is home to many fish (including some white albino catfish) and various types of plant life.

Today couples can still enjoy a cruise in those glass-bottom boats and view an underwater archaeological dig that unearthed the remains of Clovis Man, one of the hunter-gatherers who lived on the San Marcos River over 13,000 years ago.

For an overall look at the park, take a ride on the Alpine Sky Ride or up the 300-foot-tall Sky Spiral. From the Sky Spiral, you can see miles of beautiful rolling Texas Hill Country below. Recently Aquarena Springs refocused its theme from an amusement park to an environmental interpretative center. This new look includes the Natural Aquarium of Texas displaying endangered species.

You can try to see these endangered species firsthand on a tubing trip down the San Marcos. Across from Southwest Texas State University, the **Lions Club** (512-392-8255; fee) rents innertubes from May through September so that you can float down the San Marcos Loop. The floating excursion, in 72-degree water, takes about 90 minutes. Snorkeling is popular here as well, and you might see a fresh water prawn (which can reach 12 inches in length), the rare San Marcos salamander, or one of 52 kinds of fish.

Of course, not all of San Marcos's attractions are natural—plenty are of the man-made variety. However, the theme of the city as a Texas "natural" continues in many of these as well. **Downtown shops** are encouraged to feature Texas-made items. Within the last 10 years, over $16 million has been spent by the private sector in renovating the downtown area, transforming it into a shopping and dining area where visitors can see the work of Texas artists at Art Gecko, sample Texas-made brew at the Cafe on the Square Brew Pub, or select everything from Texas cigars to cookbooks at the Hill Country Humidor.

Many of the downtown businesses participate in programs sponsored by the Texas Department of Agriculture, including "Make It Texas" (featuring food and fiber of Texas), "Texas Grown" (spotlighting Texas flowers and foliage), "Naturally Texas" (highlighting fashion made with Texas fibers), "Totally Texas Menu" (featuring Texas produce, seafood, and meats in restaurants), and "Vintage Texas" (promoting Texas wines). A special San Marcos program called "Uniquely Texas" looks at the creative side of Texans, including Texas music, photos, and art.

San Marcos is well known as the home of **Southwest Texas State University,** which boasts the Southwestern Writers Collection on the seventh floor of the Alkek Library. Established in 1986 with manuscripts from the J. Frank Dobie estate, the library now contains manuscripts and working materials both about and by Texans. "This has become a premier collection of Texas writers," says Terry Toler, publications writer for Southwest Texas State University. "We have an archive of all the props from *Lonesome Dove*—everything from Gus's mummified carcass to the 'We don't rent pigs' sign. We also have the first book published about Texas," a 1526 journal by Cabeza de Vaca about his exploration of the state.

F Y I

Getting There: San Marcos is located south of Austin on I-35.

Festivals/Special Events: Ready for a bowl of red? Then head to the city of San Marcos, home of a truly Texas-sized chili cook-off with nearly 600 competitors. The activities start on Friday with college day at Chilympiad. Look for the annual Collegiate Chili Cookoff and Miss Chilympiad along with a "beefcake"—make that "chilicake"—event called Mr. Hot Stuff.

On Saturday the activities heat up again, starting with the traditional Chilympiad Parade through downtown San Marcos. Then the real work begins with the State Men's Championship Chili Cookoff, an event where the top chili cooks in the nation vie for top honors.

Historic home buffs shouldn't miss the Tours of Distinction in early May, an annual Heritage Association of San Marcos event that spotlights several of the historic homes in town. Other highlights of the weekend include Art Among the Oaks, a juried art show sponsored by the Heritage Association, the San Marcos Art League, and the River Foundation.

Shopping: Of course, San Marcos's most popular shopping stops are located alongside I-35 at exit 200. This is the location of the San Marcos Factory Shops (800-628-9465), an open-air mall featuring over 100 outlets that sell direct from the factory. Luggage, shoes, leather goods, outdoor gear, china, kitchen goods, and other specialties are offered for sale.

Just across the road, the Tanger Factory Outlet Center (512-396-7444) tempts shoppers with over 30 shops that feature name-brand designers and manufacturers. Housewares, footwear, home furnishings, leather goods, perfumes, and books are offered.

Across I-35, Centerpoint Station (512-392-1103) is a charming shop built like an old-fashioned general store. It is filled with Texas collectibles, country collectibles, T-shirts, gourmet gift foods, cookbooks, and more. Up front, a counter serves sandwiches, malts, and ice cream.

Downtown, one of the most popular and eclectic stores is the Paper Bear (214 N. LBJ Dr., 512-396-2283). Shop for Victorian stationery, silver jewelry, and more in what must rank as one of Texas's finest gift shops.

Dining: Palmer's Restaurant and Bar (RR 12 and Hutchinson, 512-353-3500; $–$$, □) offers everything from sandwiches to seafood in an atmosphere that could be described as casually elegant. Indoors, four fireplaces tempt couples, and, during warmer weather, the fountain courtyard offers alfresco dining.

Love Nests: The Texas theme even carries into the only downtown bed-and-breakfast. The Crystal River Inn (326 W. Hopkins, 512-396-3739; $–$$, □) offers visitors elegant Victorian accommodations in rooms named for Texas rivers. Owners Cathy and Mike Dillon provide guests with a selection of special packages, including tubing on the San Marcos and sunset cruises at Aquarena Springs.

But one of the most popular activities is the murder mystery weekend, a time when costumed guests work to solve a mystery using clues based on actual events in San Marcos history. The package, which includes Friday and Saturday night accommodations, begins with a welcoming party and dessert buffet where the mystery is introduced. The story features characters from San Marcos's colorful past, from wild saloon girls to unscrupulous politicians. Cast members are assigned their roles a week in advance so guests can coordinate a suitable wardrobe. The mystery spans the weekend, interrupted by river tubing in season, hayrides, or glass-bottom boat cruises, and a gourmet dinner on Saturday night. The weekend concludes on Sunday morning, when cast members solve the mystery. Mystery weekends are scheduled throughout the year.

For More Information: Give the San Marcos Convention and Visitors Bureau a call (800-782-7653 ext. 177), or while in San Marcos stop by the Tourist Information Center (exit 206 off I-35 at Aquarena Springs Dr. on the northwest side of town). Stop here for brochures on area attractions and accommodations, as well as free maps.

CADDO LAKE
Recommended for: Southern romance, fishing, quiet walks

Combine the sense of adventure in *Huck Finn* with the romance of *Gone With the Wind*. What do you have? Caddo Lake.

Located in far East Texas, this sprawling natural lake is tucked beneath a canopy of moss-draped cypress trees. Filled with the echoes of herons, the splash of 71 species of fish, and the slither of an occasional snake or alligator, Caddo Lake is like no other destination in Texas. This maze of swamp land is bursting with wildlife, flora, and the kind of romantic atmosphere you associate with the old Deep South.

Caddo Lake was once the largest natural lake in the South. This body of water is named for the Caddo Indians who once inhabited this area. They believed the lake was created by the Great Spirit. Today scientists know that the natural lake was formed by a log jam called the Great Raft on the Red River. In the 1870s the jam was cleared and the lake level dropped, ending the steamship business that once moved goods and passengers into East Texas. Today the lake has a man-made dam that keeps the lake level fairly constant (although a look at the houses built on stilts around the lake's edge will attest to its rise every decade or so).

The most popular stop in this area is **Caddo Lake State Park** (903-679-3351; admission fee). Located 14 miles northeast of Marshall on FM 2198, this 480-acre park has offered activities for both day and overnight guests since the 1930s. Stop by the visitors center for a look at displays on the lake and its playful wildlife, then travel to the picnic grounds and hiking trails.

Don't imagine Caddo Lake as an open body of water; it's a twisting, turning maze of bayous and swamps where visibility is often limited to what's just around the next bend. If you'd like to boat among these waters, you follow "boat roads," channels that wind through the trees. This is a lake for relaxation, a place to listen to wildlife or toss a fishing line. Although summer temperatures can be hot, this season can be one of the most romantic times. Dotted with hyacinths and lilies, the lake blossoms with color.

Couples who would like to camp in the park will find 48 sites. For more comfort, eight screened shelters with picnic tables (water and grill located outside) are also available. And for the ultimate in comfort, nine cabins furnished with towels, linens, kitchenettes, bathrooms with showers, air conditioners, and heat provide a romantic enclave in which to enjoy the park during the chill of winter or the heat of summer.

The lake itself lined with small communities and cabins (many with a concrete first story to prevent flood damage) that provide weekend and retirement homes. Here in the town of Uncertain you'll find accommodations like the **Caddo Cottage Bed and Breakfast** (903-789-3988 or 789-3297; $, no ☐). Located on the water's edge, this two-story cottage is fully outfitted. Check in, bring along some groceries, and make your meals in the kitchen or on the gas grill outside. Spend a romantic evening on the cottage's second-floor screened porch, where you can watch the evening fog envelop the cypress trees or hear the sound of creatures like raccoon, nutria, and beaver begin to stir.

F Y I ❧

Getting There: Caddo Lake is located in far East Texas, nearly to the Louisiana border. From Dallas, follow I-20 east to the intersection of US 59, turn north, and continue to TX 43. Turn north and continue to the small communities of Karnack and Uncertain.

Tours: One of the best ways to see this bayou country is aboard guided boat tours. The Caddo Lake Steamboat Company (903-665-1665 or 789-3978) offers day tours plus romantic moonlight and sunset cruises.

Their authentic steamboat, the *Graceful Ghost,* still operates on steam power, silently gliding through the lake waters. You may bring food and beverages aboard the 90-minute tours.

Mystique Tours (214-679-3690) travel to Big Cypress Bayou, the Big Lake area, and the swamps. Caddo Lake Tours (903-935-7579) take visitors to sites including Alligator Bayou, Hog Wallow, and Mossy Brake.

Shopping: If you want to bring home memories of Caddo, stop by the Mossy Brake Art Gallery (903-789-3414). Open afternoons except Mondays, this gallery features the work of local artists who have captured the special atmosphere of the lake in oil, watercolor, and other media.

Dining: Catfish lovers should also save time for a meal at The Catfish Cottage and Steak house (903-789-3333; $–$$, □). Be prepared to wait for a plate of golden fried catfish accompanied by coleslaw and a baked potato in one of the area's most popular restaurants.

For More Information: Contact the Northeast Texas Tourism Council, P.O. Box 949, Pittsburg, TX 75686.

WIMBERLEY
Recommended for: shopping, swimming, country getaways

Texans know there's only one sure way to cool off in the heat of the summer—head to water. No man-made air conditioner has ever been as relieving as a dip in a shady swimming hole. And one of the best swimming spots in the state is located northeast of San Antonio in the community of Wimberley.

Tucked in the rolling hills lies **Blue Hole Recreation Club** (follow Cypress Creek Rd. and turn left at the cemetery onto Blue Hole Rd., 512-847-9127; admission fee), a family-owned park that's been a favorite swimming hole with Texans since the pioneer days. One look at this pristine park and it's easy to see the reasons for this site's popularity. The swimming hole itself is a deep spot on Cypress Creek, a chilly, spring-fed creek that flows right through downtown Wimberley. Its banks are shaded with majestic cypress trees, whose sturdy trunks have served as ladders for generations of divers and whose delicately leafed branches have shaded innumerable picnickers.

This park has been in operation since 1928. The property was owned by the Dobie family, whose nearby home now serves as a popular bed-and-breakfast. A friend of the Dobies offered to pay for a road to the swimming hole, and soon after the site was opened to the public. Throughout the years, the spot has been considered one of the finest swimming holes in Texas. It's such a typical Texas swimming spot, in fact, that it's been sought out by the movie industry, playing a part in *Honeysuckle Rose* and *Small Town in Texas*.

Today Blue Hole is still a family operation, with hand-lettered signs and meticulously maintained grounds. It operates as a recreation club, with daily, weekly, monthly, and seasonal memberships. Memberships range from $5 to $50 per family, and members pay a daily entrance fee of $1 per person.

Camping is also available at Blue Hole. Rustic campsites with picnic tables are located directly on the banks of Cypress Creek. RV camping, with water and electricity (and sewer hook-ups at some sites), is available a short distance from the water.

Whether you come picnicking for the day or camping for a vacation, you'll find it hard to tear yourself away from the beauty of this swimming hole. Children swing Tarzan-style from metal rings attached to stately cypress trees before dropping into the chilly 13-foot depths below. Younger brothers and sisters wade in the ankle-deep waters nearby, sifting through the gravel bottom for a pretty rock. Snorkelers seek out perch and bass in the water's depths, easily visible in the clear creek water.

Although it's difficult to tear yourself away from Blue Hole, you'll also find many attractions in **Wimberley,** just a mile from the popular swimming spot. This shop-'til-you-drop town is filled with stores offering antiques, collectibles, one-of-a-kind clothing, jewelry, and art. Many of the shops are located on the square, so budget a couple of hours to walk from store to store.

Whether you're coming to Wimberley to swim or shop—or to sample a little of both—you've found a perfect summer getaway. Take the plunge!

F Y I 〜

Getting There: Wimberley is located between Austin and San Antonio. From I-35, turn west on RR 12 and continue to the Hill Country community.

Festivals/Special Events: You'll also find plenty of shopping during Wimberley Market Days, held the first Saturday of each month from April through December. This popular show draws 400 vendors and thousands of shoppers.

Love Nests: Wimberley is also home to many bed-and-breakfast accommodations offering visitors a chance to stay in a historic home, along the river, or at a local ranch. For information on these many accommodations, give one of the reservation services a call: Country Innkeepers (800-230-0805), Hill Country Accommodations (800-926-5028), or Wimberley Lodging Reservation Service (800-460-3909). For brochures on Wimberley's other accommodations, call the Chamber of Commerce at (512) 847-2201.

For More Information: Contact the Chamber of Commerce at (512) 847-2201. For more on Blue Hole, call (512) 847-9127.

NEW BRAUNFELS
Recommended for: water park, tubing, shopping

When the hot summer sun beats down on the Lone Star State, Texans head to New Braunfels. Less than an hour south of Austin, this German community is filled with water sports ranging from wading to white-water rafting, guaranteed to cure those hot weather blues.

The land that is now New Braunfels was first called "The Fountains" by local Indians because of its crystal clear springs. These springs drew the city's founder, Prince Carl of the Solms-Braunfels region of Germany, to the area in 1845. With his group of immigrant farmers, the prince began the community of New Braunfels, named for his homeland. The leader never quite got over his fear of Indian attack: he insisted on wearing an iron vest for security every day!

The city of 25,000 residents has never forgotten these ties to the old country. German is the main language in many local homes, and every fall the town hosts Wurstfest, one of the largest German festivals in the country. But during the summer months, it's water, not wurst, that's king in this Hill Country community. New Braunfels boasts two recreational rivers—the Comal and the Guadalupe—the largest water park in the state, glass-bottom boat cruises, waterskiing, rafting, inner tubing, canoeing, and more ways to beat the heat.

The beautiful **Comal River** holds the title as the world's shortest river. It may be small, but the Comal packs a lot into its two miles. The headwaters are the **Comal Springs,** one of the largest springs in the state. Downstream, the river flows through **Landa Park,** a 300-acre center for family picnics and gatherings. Cool off with a dip in the park's 1.2-million-gallon swimming pool, fed with spring water. There's a glass-bottom boat ride nearby where you can have a look at the varied aquatic life.

Tubers also enjoy a thrilling ride through "The Chute" in **Prince Solms Park.** To maneuver around the dam in the river, part of the Comal is diverted through the chute, where tubers of all ages enjoy a breathtaking swoosh from the deeper water above the dam to the shallower water below.

You can also enjoy the Comal at **Schlitterbahn** (305 W. Austin St., 210-625-2351; admission fee), which means "slippery road" in German. This resort and waterpark takes its beauty from the natural-looking, man-made rides and from the Comal River, which supplies 24,000 gallons of spring water to the park every minute. "Schlitterbahn is the only water park in the country designed around a spring-fed river," says Jana Wilkinson, director of marketing for the popular park. "It's a unique natural setting that really sets us apart from most water parks."

This is also the largest tubing park in the nation, with nine manmade chutes. It has rides for every age, from the steep 60-foot "Schlittercoaster" and the mile-long "Raging River" tube chute for daredevils to a 50,000-gallon hot tub with a swim-up bar for the less adventurous. You're welcome to bring along a picnic and enjoy the tables scattered throughout the park and along the riverbanks.

New Braunfels is also home a much longer recreational river, the Guadalupe, one very popular with inner tubers, rafters, and canoeists.

They find miles of cypress-shaded river that includes straight, calm stretches for families and beginners, as well as white water for thrill seekers.

The waters of the Comal are cool, but the **Guadalupe River** is downright chilly. With an average water temperature in the mid-50s, it still doesn't deter tubers who frequent the businesses that line the River Road, a scenic drive that winds for miles along the riverbanks.

For just a few dollars, a river outfitter will set you up with an inner tube and take you to one of the drop-off points on the Guadalupe. From there, you can drift downstream for hours. Many tubers carry along an ice chest, tied to a tube, and spend a half day with their legs dangling in the cool, emerald green waters. The outfitter will meet you at a predetermined point at the end of your journey.

When you're ready to dry off, you'll find that New Braunfels has a host of historic, shopping, and dining opportunities. Collectors of the popular Hummel figurines shouldn't miss the 15,000-square-foot **Hummel Museum** (199 Main Plaza, 800-456-4866; admission fee). The museum chronicles the life of German nun Sister Maria Innocentia Hummel through her sketches, paintings, and personal diaries. It's filled with 350 original paintings and early sketches that spawned the popular Hummel figurines, plates, and other collectibles.

Whatever your interests, grab your swimsuit and sunscreen and head for New Braunfels. And, unlike Prince Solms, feel free to leave your iron vest at home. You'll find the natives are very friendly.

F Y I ✎

Getting There: New Braunfels is located on I-35 approximately 30 miles north of San Antonio.

Nearby Attractions: Plant lovers should stop by the Lindheimer Home (491 Comal Ave.; admission fee). Located on the banks of the Comal River, this home belonged to Ferdinand Lindheimer, a botanist who lent his name to over 30 Texas plant species. Now restored, it contains early memorabilia from Lindheimer's career as both botanist and newspaper publisher. A backyard garden is filled with examples of his native flora discoveries.

Another popular stop is Natural Bridge Caverns (for more information see the "Adventures for Two" chapter of this book). Adjacent to the cave lies Natural Bridge Wildlife Ranch (210-438-7400; admission fee). The drive through the ranch takes you past zebras, gazelles, antelopes, and ostriches, and feeding is allowed.

Shopping: New Braunfels calls itself the antique capital of Texas, and it has plenty of shops to back up that claim. Check out the Downtowner I Antique Mall (223 W. San Antonio St., off the Plaza, 210-629-3947) for every kind of antique imaginable. For collectibles, visit Opa's Haus (1600 River Rd., 1/2 mile north of Loop 337, 210-629-1191). Opa's Haus operates a secondary or resale market for limited-edition collectibles. The store sells plates, steins, ornaments, and cuckoo clocks as well as Hummel figurines.

The New Braunfels Factory Stores (exits 187 and 189 off I-35, 210-620-6806) are among the most popular stops in town.

Dining: You wouldn't expect to find fine continental dining in a small town, but that's what makes Wolfgang's Keller (295 E. San Antonio St., 210-625-9169; $$, □) so special. Located in the cellar of the Prince Solms Inn (see "Love Nests"), this restaurant has long been a favorite with New Braunfels couples looking for a place to celebrate a special occasion. Start with an appetizer of blue fin crab cakes and move on to the charbroiled rib eye, filet with wild mushroom sauce, or herb-crusted chicken. This is truly an elegant restaurant for a reasonable price.

Love Nests: To feel like you've left the 20th century, get away for a weekend at Prince Solms Inn (295 E. San Antonio St., 210-625-9169; $, □). Built at the turn of the century, this quiet bed-and-breakfast has two suites and a guest parlor downstairs; upstairs there are eight guest rooms. All rooms are furnished with period antiques. If you like mysteries, consider a stay during one of the murder mystery weekends. Guests spend the weekend sleuthing, and the case is revealed during Sunday's breakfast.

Another favorite of ours is the Faust Hotel (240 S. Seguin Ave., 210-625-7791; $, □). A New Braunfels tradition, this 1929 four-story, renovated hotel features a bar that's popular with locals and visitors. The lobby is appointed with beautiful antique furnishings.

For More Information: Call the New Braunfels Convention and Visitors Bureau at (800) 572-2626.

SHOP 'TIL
YOU (BOTH) DROP

SOMETIMES THERE'S NO MORE RELAXING
activity than a day spent leisurely shopping together,
walking from store to store, admiring window displays,
and looking for unique items. Following is a peek at several "shop 'til you drop" burgs where shopping is the
hottest thing in town. Most feature small boutique shops
with Texas-made items, antiques, and art.

CANTON
Recommended for: flea market shopping

"It's here somewhere," the dealer called out to a woman wandering from booth to booth, searching the tables of merchandise for a special item. "I know it is!" the customer replied, before heading off to the next antiques-filled row.

And in all likelihood, it was there some-where. Whether "it" was a Madame Alexander doll, a Gene Autry lunchbox, an 1800s oak trunk, or an advertising sign, it's probably for sale at **First Monday Trade Days** in Canton. Every month, this tiny East Texas community of 3,000 swells with over 150,000 shoppers looking for a bargain or a hard-to-find item to add to their collection. Over 5,000 dealers offer everything from garage sale items to fine antiques in an atmosphere that's part carnival, part flea market, and all fun.

"If we don't have it in Canton, you don't need it or it's not made," says Joe Collins, executive director of the Canton Chamber of Commerce. The city has been long been reaping the benefits of this Texas-sized flea market. Trade Days is the town's largest industry, spilling $2 million annually into the city coffers. The result: no property tax for Canton residents, a new sewer system, a new civic center, and prosperous motels and bed-and-breakfast inns.

First Mondays dates back to 1873 when court was held on the first Monday of the month. To pass the time while waiting for the judge, the townspeople began to do some trading, swapping a goat for a quilt or a pair of wagon wheels for a load of hay. After a while, trade days became a regular event on the courthouse square. For nearly a century, the practice continued and grew. Finally in 1965, the city of Canton decided to relocate the monthly swap meet to grounds two blocks north of the courthouse. With more room as well as promotion and organization by the city, the popularity of the trade days soared.

Today both buyers and sellers come from all over the country to attend the monthly market. The sale takes place over the four days preceding the first Monday of each month. Many vendors arrive by RV (traveling 60 miles east of Dallas to Canton on I-20) and begin setting up on Wednesday. No sales can be made before Thursday, informally known as "Dealer's Day." Vendors wheel and deal on this day, but sales are open to the public. Thursday is a good time to arrive to beat the crowds and to have first chance at the bargains.

On Friday, Trade Days really swings into action as over 100 acres of parking fills with cars from around Texas and neighboring states. Parking is $3 for the day or $2 in remote lots. The sale picks up speed on Saturday and Sunday. Most dealers begin to pack up on Sunday evening, but some die-hard traders remain until Monday.

Many dealers return month after month, so some shoppers quickly head to the "Doll Lady's" booth or the "Marble Man's" tables. The atmosphere among the dealers is like a family gathering. "They're just like kinfolks," explains Joe Collins. "For a lot of them, it's like a reunion to come back to Canton. They do a lot of trading and swapping among themselves."

That family spirit carries over in the dealers' interactions with shoppers. Talk is free-flowing, with advice on collectibles given out gladly. Dealers and shoppers swap stories and enjoy good-natured bartering, an accepted practice among most of the vendors.

Wear good walking shoes at the Trade Days because of the uneven paths and the magnitude of the grounds. And don't plan to see everything, even if you stay for the weekend. Booths sprawl endlessly across the East Texas landscape, so save some areas for your next visit.

Besides the open-air market, Canton now has **covered pavilions,** areas set up with crafts and furniture-filled booths. Look here for refinished ice boxes, sideboards, bureaus, and more. A new **civic center** also provides enclosed vendor space. If you purchase large items anywhere on the grounds, the dealer can provide you with a special driving permit to allow you to bring your car around and load up.

Food concessions are sprinkled throughout the market, filling the air with the scent of sugar-coated funnel cakes, spicy Navajo tacos, or smoky Texas barbecue.

No matter what your collecting interest, you'll probably find it here at Canton—somewhere. And, as every collector knows, the search is half the fun, especially when it's conducted among 5,000 dealers in this East Texas hamlet.

F Y I ✎

Getting There: Canton is located 40 miles from Tyler, the rose capital of the nation.

Love Nests: Make plans early to stay in the town's relatively few motel rooms. Surrounding towns such as Athens and Tyler swell with overnight guests clamoring for a hotel bed. Canton's 30 bed-and-breakfast properties have become another increasingly popular option for travelers. For a brochure listing accommodations, contact the Chamber of Commerce.

For More Information: Contact the Chamber of Commerce at 1001 N. Trade Days Blvd., Canton, TX 75103, or call (903) 567-2991. Ask for a calendar of "First Mondays Trade Days" and a list of motels and bed-and-breakfasts in the area. If you're interested in selling as well as buying, the Chamber has a special brochure for vendors.

SALADO

Recommended for: antiques shopping, dining, B&Bs

This quiet community is located where Salado Creek flows beneath I-35. This site was once a stagecoach stop on the old Chisholm Trail and served the line that stretched from San Antonio to Little Rock.

Today the Chisholm Trail has long been replaced by the busy interstate system, but the stagecoach stop atmosphere of this small community remains—as does the stagecoach stop itself. Today it's called the **Stagecoach Inn,** and offers accommodations in a modern addition. The original building, where Sam Houston once delivered an antisecession speech, is now an elegant restaurant. The old stretch of stagecoach route is now Main Street, lined with antique shops and specialty stores, many housed in historic structures. In all, 18 buildings are listed in the National Register of Historic Places, and 23 boast Texas Historical Markers.

This community is a shopping stop for interstate travelers on their way from Dallas to Austin or San Antonio. Antique stores, artists' galleries, and specialty shops fill the historic downtown buildings. We enjoy spending an afternoon in Salado, browsing through shops like **Salado Galleries** (Main St. across from the Stagecoach Inn, 817-947-5110), which sells fine art, including many bluebonnet paintings of

Central Texas fields. We've also bought many gifts at **Salado Pottery** (beside the Stagecoach Inn, 817-947-5935), offering beautiful Salado-made pottery, from water pitchers to bird feeders.

Across the street, the **Shady Villa** (Main St.) is an open-air mini-mall that sells everything from unique kaleidoscopes and collectibles to Victorian jewelry and gifts from around the world. We also found a little bit of everything at **The Women's Exchange** (N. Main St. at Salado Creek, 817-947-5552), built in 1860. This structure has served as a drugstore, law office, stagecoach stop, and Salado's only saloon, but today it's filled with antiques and collectibles.

Perhaps the best-known shop in town is the **Grace Jones Shop** (1 Royal St., 817-947-5555). You wouldn't expect to find the latest New York fashions in a Texas town of little more than 1,000 residents, but here it is. The store's owner, Grace Jones (not the actress), was once a fashion model. Another popular stop is **Sir Wigglesworth** (Rock Creek at Main St., 817-947-8846). Glass and ceramics, antique linens, baskets of every shape, and concrete animals from pigs to ducks are just a few of the items that crowd this store.

If the shopping has the two of you tired out, relax with a massage at **Salado Beauty Spa** (6 N. Main St., 817-947-9360). This spa specializes in European facials, full body and back massages, Egyptian foot massages, and more.

Finally, unwind at **Pace Park** (downtown, just off Main St.; free). This beautiful area is filled with tall oaks and is an excellent spot to bring a picnic lunch and wade in the creek. Don't miss the statue of Sirena, located in the middle of the creek just behind the Grace Jones Shop. Local artist Troy Kelley sculpted the statue cast in bronze of the legendary Indian maiden who was transformed into a mermaid by a magical fish. Mornings you can see steam rising from the chilly waters of the pure springs near the statue.

For the most romantic ride around Salado, check out **Johnson Carriage Service** (Main St. across from the Stagecoach Inn, 817-939-7519; fee). On Friday and weekend evenings, the carriage winds down Main Street for a leisurely look at the historic town. The carriage service is also available for weddings and special occasions.

F Y I 〰

Getting There: Salado is located on I-35, about 50 miles south of Waco.

Dining: When we're looking for a romantic dinner, we've often headed off to the Stagecoach Inn (I-35, east side, 817-947-5111; $$–$$$, ☐). This elegant restaurant features waitresses who come to your table and recite the day's offerings by heart. Entrees include chicken-fried steak, baked ham, whole catfish, roast prime rib of beef, and T-bone steak. Don't miss the hush puppies or the banana fritters.

Love Nests: The best-known accommodation in town is the Stagecoach Inn (I-35, east side, 817-947-5111; $–$$, ☐). This reminder of Salado's early days started out as the Shady Villa Inn, an important rest stop on the Chisholm Trail. Today the accommodations are housed in a modern addition, and the original building, where Sam Houston once delivered an antisecession speech, is now an elegant restaurant. Its notable guests included General George Custer, Robert E. Lee, and outlaw Jesse James.

For more intimate lodgings, consider The Inn at Salado (N. Main St. at Pace Park, 817-947-8200; $–$$, ☐). This elegant white two-story bed-and-breakfast is located in the main shopping district. Room rates include a full breakfast.

Another romantic spot is The Inn on the Creek (Circle Center, 817-947-5554; $–$$, ☐). Located just off Salado Creek, this inn is actually a collection of five houses that have been elegantly restored. The oldest portion of the inn was constructed in 1892 and later moved to this site. Guests can select from 16 double rooms with baths or a cottage suite.

For More Information: Call the Salado Chamber of Commerce at (817) 947-5040.

GRUENE
Recommended for: shopping, river rafting, music

A 46-star U.S. flag hangs over a steamy dance hall, where the only air conditioning is a breeze through the wide front door. Advertisements from the 1930s decorate the walls. Burlap bags, suspended from the ceiling, dampen the sounds of shuffling feet and country-western bands.

Although it may sound like another Hollywood version of small town life in

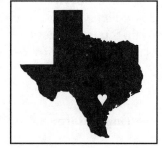

Texas, this is **Gruene Hall,** the oldest dance hall in the Lone Star State. Since the 1878, this joint has shaken to the sounds of Texas music—from gutbucket country to folk to blues. Over the years, the dance and music styles may have changed, but Gruene Hall, like a good pair of boots, has remained as dependable as ever.

This dance hall is located in Gruene, north of New Braunfels off Interstate 35. Like Waxahachie and Refugio, the pronunciation of Gruene is one of those things that sets a real Texan apart. To sound like a local, just say "Green" when referring to this weekend destination.

Tucked under tall live oaks near the banks of the Guadalupe River, today Gruene is a "shop-'til-you-drop" kind of town, filled with antique stores and boutiques, alfresco restaurants, and historic buildings. The hamlet is quiet on weekdays, but on Friday afternoons the streets fill with shoppers, river rafters and tubers, and city folks looking for a small town weekend escape.

Gruene's days have not always been so prosperous. The town was started in the 1870s by H. D. Gruene at a time when cotton was king. With its swinging dance hall and busy cotton gin, prosperity reigned until the boll weevil arrived in Texas with the Great Depression right on its heels. Gruene's foreman hanged himself from the water tower, and H. D.'s plans for the town withered like the cotton in the fields. The community became a ghost town.

One hundred years after its founding, investors began restoring Gruene's historic buildings and, little by little, businesses began moving into the once-deserted structures. Gruene was placed on the National Register of Historic Places. Today all the downtown structures are filled with thriving establishments that range from restaurants to a potter to a general store. The commercial area of Gruene is a T-shape formed by Gruene and Hunter Roads.

The **Gruene General Store** (1610 Hunter Rd., 210-629-6021) brings back memories of small town life during Gruene's heyday as a cotton center. This was the first mercantile store, built in 1878 to serve the families that worked on the cotton farms. It also served as a stage-coach stop and a post office. Today instead of farm implements and dry goods, however, this 1990s general store sells cookbooks, fudge, and Texas-themed clothing and sodas from an old-fashioned fountain.

As the population of Gruene rose, so did the need for merchandise, and in 1904 the general store moved to a new brick building. This was once the biggest store in Comal County, selling everything from lamp oil to caskets. Today the **Gruene Antique Company** (1607 Hunter

Rd., 210-629-7781) fills this huge building with the wares of numerous vendors. Nearby, **Lone Star Country Goods** (1613 Hunter Rd., 210-609-1613) sells cowboy kitsch, with everything from lamps to dinnerware.

For one-of-a-kind items, visit **Buck Pottery** (1296 Gruene Rd., 210-629-7975). Here Dee and Terry Buck are usually hard at work on their stoneware pottery, blending and kneading several types of clay and then, with the aid of a potter's wheel, shaping it into creations that range from plates to pitchers. During the firing at 2,400 degrees for 16 to 18 hours, the pottery receives a coat of wood ash created by two cords of wood consumed during the process. The final result: one-of-a-kind pottery, glazed by the wood ash that collects and melts on each piece.

You'll also find handmade items at **Bushwhacker's** (1633 Hunter Rd., 210-620-4534 or 800-676-4534). Handmade swings, coffee tables, and other furniture are crafted from cypress and mesquite at this shop.

In the summer, cool off after all that shopping with a relaxing float down the Guadalupe River. The **Rockin' R River Rides** (1405 Gruene Rd., 210-629-9999 or 800-55-FLOAT) and **Gruene River Company** (1495 Gruene Rd., 210-625-2800) take visitors of all abilities—from families to daredevils—to one of the drop-off points on the Guadalupe. From there, you can drift beneath the tall cypress trees for hours.

F Y I ✍

Getting There: From San Antonio, take I-35 north about 30 miles. Take exit 191 and head left for 1-1/2 miles, then turn left at the light. Continue for a mile to Gruene.

Festivals/Special Events: Ever since we all watched Demi Moore and Patrick Swayze molding clay in *Ghost,* pottery making brings up sensual images for many of us. If that's the case, you might go into overload at the Texas Clay Festival, held every October on the grounds of Buck Pottery. Admission is free to the event, which features 20 potters from around the state demonstrating their craft.

Although there's always plenty going on in town, Gruene really springs to life during Market Days, the third weekend of every month from February through November. This arts-and-crafts festival attracts more than 100 vendors from across the state and shoppers from central and south Texas who come to look for everything from handmade furniture to hot sauces. Admission to the festival is free.

Dining: So that no one actually does shop until they drop, Gruene features several excellent restaurants. If it's barbecue you crave, stop by Guadalupe Smoked Meat Company (1299 Gruene Rd., 210-629-6121; $$, ☐). Owner Janie Macredie was one of the first investors who started pumping life back in this former ghost town. She opened the Guadalupe Smoked Meat Company in the old Rodriguez Family General store, a historic building moved to Gruene from the community of Martindale, and set about serving some of the tenderest brisket in Central Texas.

Located on the banks of the Guadalupe River, the Grist Mill Restaurant (1287 Gruene Rd., 210-625-0684; $$, ☐) is housed in the ruins of a 100-year-old cotton gin. In the early days, an explosion blew a hole in the side of the building that today serves fried chicken, chicken-fried steak, and other Texas favorites. You can eat inside or outside on the deck overlooking the Guadalupe River.

Gruene Hall: Texas's oldest dance hall opens at 11 a.m. most days (noon on Sundays). On weekdays, there's usually no cover charge for evening performances. Weekend cover charges vary with performer. For information, call (210) 606-1281.

Love Nests: Guests at the Gruene Mansion Inn (1275 Gruene Rd., 210-629-2641; $$, no ☐) stay in restored 1870 cottages on a bluff overlooking the Guadalupe River. A two-night rental is required on weekends.

For More Information: Call the Gruene Information Center at (210) 629-5077, or the New Braunfels Convention and Visitors Bureau at (800) 572-2626.

ROUND TOP
Recommended for: shopping, country getaways, B&Bs, music, history

Imagine starting your day in a two-story cabin. You and your loved one are snuggled beneath a down comforter in an attic room lit with windows that have seen a century of Texas sunrises. After a country breakfast, you sit on the porch and watch as Texas's smallest town slowly wakes up. Later that day, you shop for antiques, tour a historic village, then dine on shrimp marinara or grilled red

snapper. Finally, the day draws to an end with a production of Shake-speare, performed in a barn deep in the Texas countryside.

This is Round Top, population 81. A favorite getaway for Houstonians, this village is a marriage of country charm and city culture, a place where you can bicycle on quiet backroads and enjoy a concert by a world-class pianist in a grand hall reminiscent of a European cathedral, all in the same day.

Round Top is also a shopping hotspot for Texans who are looking for quality antiques and a country getaway. They park their cars downtown and enjoy walking from shop to shop; almost every store is located on the square or just one block away. One of the longest running shops on the square is the **Round Top General Store** (409-249-3600). Since 1848, this two-story structure has met the needs of Round Top area residents by serving as a hardware store, grocery store, barber shop, funeral home, and even a hotel. Today it's a shop once again, but one specializing in antiques and collectibles.

You'll also find plenty of antiques at **Daisy Antiques** (409-249-3142). Look for loads of Texas furniture here, especially primitives, as well as baby cradles, baby beds, and even Victrolas among the inventory.

Old book lovers should head to **Round Top Relics** (409-249-5504). This store specializes in books and magazines and also has a wonderful selection of wardrobes and china cabinets.

At the **Porch Office** (409-249-5594) owner Sherry Peck has just about a little of everything—primitive cabinets, antique picture frames, iron beds, cutaway linens and quilts, and you name it. Almost all of her merchandise is from Texas. This shop is open Thursday through Sunday.

Round Top is best known as the home of **Festival Hill** (TX 237, 5 blocks north of Henkel Square, 409-249-3129; admission fee), the brainchild of pianist James Dick. Started about 25 years ago, this center serves as a training ground every summer for serious music students from around the world, selected to live and study here under the direction of a world-class faculty. Their work has brought universal recognition, including a 13-hour series recorded and distributed through National Public Radio.

The focal point of Festival Hill is the concert hall, a 1,000-seat limestone structure whose interior, when not hosting a concert, is still a construction zone. In its grandiose scale and its dedication to craftsmanship, the concert hall rises from its rural surroundings like a grand cathedral looming above a European town. Work on the concert hall and the rest of Festival Hill is on a "pay as you go" basis. Carpenters recreate Old World craftsmanship slowly, with projects such as a ceiling filled with compass stars, each composed of over 700 pieces of beaded board.

"This woodwork and the creation of it is something that can still be done today," explains James Dick. "You can still aspire to do something with your hands. That's what Festival Hill is—doing something with your hands and doing something that blooms out of that endeavor."

Even if you don't have the opportunity to attend a concert, call to schedule a tour of the building. Your look at Festival Hill can include the David Guion Museum Room, housing a collection of belongings and music of this Texas composer, and the Oxehufwud Room, a collection of Swedish decorative arts which recalls the life of a Swedish noble family whose final member retired in La Grange.

But when there's no concert, the most romantic activity at Festival Hill is picnicking. Bring a picnic lunch and enjoy the 100-acre grounds, planted with thousands of trees and crossed by walking trails and a recently completed stonework bridge, constructed to resemble a Roman footbridge. Tucked beneath tall oaks, the grounds are quiet and you'll usually dine without disturbance.

Another well-known area stop is the **Winedale Historic Center** (4 miles north of Round Top on FM 1457, north on FM 2714, 409-278-3530; admission fee). Operated by the University of Texas, this site hosts annual Shakespeare productions. A cast of students from assorted disciplines have come to Winedale every summer for the past two decades to perform the works of the Bard in an old hay barn. For 15 to 18 hours a day, the students make costumes, prepare lighting, and practice, practice, practice. Public performances are held Thursday through Sunday evenings in late July and early August.

Although Shakespeare at Winedale is only a summer-only activity, the historic center is a year-round attraction. Winedale is the creation of the late philanthropist Miss Ima Hogg, daughter of former Governor James Hogg. The project began in 1964 and was donated to the University of Texas three years later. Today the 215-acre complex houses a collection of historic structures, a research center, a nature trail, and a picnic area. Weekend tours take visitors through homes furnished with period antiques and boasting features such as stenciled ceilings that recall the German culture of the area.

You can also get a glimpse into the lifestyle of the area's earlier residents at **Henkel Square** (on the square, 409-249-3308; admission fee), a collection of historic structures. The 40 buildings of Henkel Square were assembled from around Fayette County and include an apothecary shop that now serves as a visitors center, a schoolhouse-church, and a log house whose walls are tinted with wash bluing. The preservation of the buildings and the thousands of artifacts with which they are filled is due to the early residents of Round Top.

From Shakespeare to shopping, Beethoven to bed-and-breakfasts, Round Top offers big city culture with small town simplicity.

F Y I ✎

Getting There: Round Top is located northwest of Houston. Travel west on US 290 to the intersection of TX 237 (west of Brenham). Turn south on TX 237 and continue for eight miles.

Festivals/Special Events: Although shopping in Round Top is good on any weekend, twice a year it's so good that it draws shoppers from around the country. These are the weekends of the Round Top Antiques Fair, when over 200 dealers bring their wares to this small town. This show is held the first weekends in April and October. Often called the best antique show in Texas, the three-day fair focuses on American country antiques.

This show began as a way for 22 antique dealers to add to their collections. For nearly three decades the show has continued to grow and word of its uniqueness has spread. Every dealer is required to bring fresh merchandise to his booth—items not shown in previous shows. Booths offer everything from teddy bears to Windsor chairs, quilts to majolica, tole to tinware. Other exhibitors offer American Indian rugs, rods, reels, creels, lodge furniture, country wicker, and baskets.

In recent years the fair has added displays in an air-conditioned dance hall, so now the show includes booths featuring decorative arts, more formal furniture, Tiffany silver, Staffordshire, antique Oriental rugs, Flow Blue, and other fineries.

The Round Top Antiques Fair combines with the Round Top Folk Art Fair as the overflow of antique dealers sets up with folk artisans on Highway 237. The Folk Art Fair is a real bonanza for collectors of folk dolls, vintage buttons, woodcarvings, needlework, and more. All the fair participants are selected because they work in Colonial and traditional styles, so their work is not at all like what you would see in a typical arts-and-crafts show. They have been chosen because their work complements the "country antiques" look featured in the show.

Admission to the show is good for all three days, and there are no early sales, so every shopper has an equal chance.

Dining: Royer's Round Top Cafe (on the square, 409-249-3611; $$, □) is a country cafe with surprisingly sophisticated entrees such as grilled red snapper and pasta with fresh marinara and shrimp. It's open Friday and Saturday for lunch and dinner, Sunday for late lunch.

Love Nests: In keeping with the historic emphasis of the town's attractions and shops, Round Top's many bed-and-breakfast operations have an old-fashioned, small town flair. Visitors at the Round Top Inn (TX 237, 409-249-5294; $–$$, □) stay in historic structures. These 19th-century buildings each have 20th-century comforts, including air conditioning, central heating, and private baths. The inn spans a city block, formerly the property of Johann Traugott Wandke, an herbalist and organ maker who is known to have hand-crafted seven pipe organs from local cedar during his residence here. (His home is part of the inn; his stone workshop now houses an herb shop.)

Bed-and-breakfast lovers looking for a slightly different atmosphere appreciate Heart of My Heart Ranch (CR 217, 800-327-1242; $–$$, □), located about two miles from town. Heart of My Heart has nine rooms, all containing antique furnishings. Guests can enjoy a taste of country life, fish in the stocked lake, bicycle country backroads, or just sit out on the grounds and listen to the sounds of the ranch's cattle herd.

For More Information: Write the Round Top Merchants Association, Round Top, TX 78954, or call (409) 249-4042.

GLADEWATER
Recommended for: antiques shopping, arts and crafts

The community of Gladwater calls itself "The Antique Capital of East Texas." One look around this community, located northeast of Tyler, and it's easy to see why. Sixteen antique malls, 200 antique dealers, and an atmosphere conducive to a day of shopping for that long-sought item make this a true shopper's dream.

Gladewater's early days were equally rich—but in a far different way. A point on the Texas and Pacific Railroad line, the town hit "black gold" in the early 1930s, making the small community a boomtown. When the first gusher blew in, the town's population blew as well—rising from 500 to 10,000 in a short time. Gladewater became the capital of East Texas's oil industry, with five refineries and 400 oil wells within the city. Two oil wells were even drilled in **Rosedale Cemetery** (Hwy. 80 and Loop 281), and it became known as "the world's richest cemetery."

Like it did across much of Texas, however, the boom turned to bust in the 1980s. Wells were capped; refineries closed. But Gladewater turned to another source of riches: antiques.

Today, enjoy shopping for just about any collectible item or antique at the town's many malls and shops. Check out **Antiques II** (112 N. Main St., 903-845-6493), **Gladewater Antique Mall** (100 E. Commerce, 903-845-4440), and **St. Claire Antique Emporium** (104 W. Pacific, 903-845-4079).

F Y I &

Getting There: Gladewater is located at the intersection of US 80 and US 271, just north of I-20.

Festivals/Special Events: Gladewater parties year-round with special events like East Texas Gusher Days in late April. Recalling the city's early boom days, this festival includes a street dance, arts and crafts, a chili cook-off, and more. In late May, put on your bobby socks and head over to the Fifties Fest with antiques and collectibles plus live entertainment.

You'll find lots of browsing and shopping opportunities at the Annual Arts and Crafts Festival in late September. Over 200 exhibitors from surrounding states make this the largest outdoor arts and crafts festival in East Texas.

Dining: One of the most popular spots in the Gladewater area is Annie's Tea Room (TX 155 N. in Big Sandy, 903-636-4355; $-$$, □). Part of a complex of Victorian buildings that make up Annie's Bed and Breakfast (see "Love Nests"), the tea room serves a lot more than tea and scones: order up steak, low-cal entrees, and more.

Love Nests: Annie's Bed and Breakfast (TX 155 N. in Big Sandy, 800-BB-ANNIE; $–$$, ☐) is a destination in itself for many East Texas travelers. The creation of Annie Potter, a local crafter whose needlecraft business became a multimillion dollar industry, guests here can choose from 12 double rooms (7 with private baths). All rooms are housed in renovated Victorian homes and decorated with period furnishings.

For More Information: Call the Gladewater Chamber of Commerce at (903) 845-5501.

COZY
COMMUNITIES

A CHANCE TO RELAX. TO SIT OUT ON A FRONT porch rocker or walk to town. To have folks remember your name even though you've been in town less than 24 hours. To be not a room number but a guest. This is small town Texas, a place where Texas friendly can be witnessed on a daily basis. Many of these communities offer accommodations in bed-and-breakfast homes, where you'll be feeling like part of the family before the day's end.

BASTROP
Recommended for: shopping, piney woods

According to Indian legend, the Lost Pines of Bastrop were a gift from a brave to his new bride, homesick for East Texas. Scientists provide a less romantic explanation: The coniferous trees were left in Central Texas when a shallow sea receded 80 million years ago. A prehistoric forest thrived across much of the state, but when conditions changed only an island of loblolly pines remained.

Regardless of the explanation, one thing's for certain—the Lost Pines are far from lost. This forest enclave southeast of Austin is found by over 600,000 guests annually. Today **Bastrop State Park** (TX 21, 1-1/2 miles east of town, 512-321-2101; admission fee) is one of the most visited parks in the Lone Star State. Some of the most popular features of the park are the cabins, built by the Civilian Conservation Corps in the late 1930s. Two work companies came to the newly created park to plant pine seedlings and to construct buildings using native red sandstone. Paid about a dollar a day, these skilled craftsmen left a legacy of rustic-style cabins furnished with hand-crafted tables and carved fireplace mantels.

Bastrop State Park also boasts a 365,000-gallon swimming pool and a nine-hole golf course that's consistently cited as one of the top two public courses in the state. But for all its man-made attractions, this park is even richer in natural treasures. Fishermen enjoy a 10-acre lake stocked with bass and catfish. Birdwatchers seek out pine siskins, pileated woodpeckers, and painted buntings. Hikers walk a quiet eight-and-a-half-mile trail, the sounds of campers and picnickers dampened by a carpet of pine needles.

Bastrop State Park neighbors **Buescher** (pronounced "Bisher") **State Park** (Park Rd. 1, 512-237-2241; admission fee), but the two present different environments. The number of pine trees diminishes as you head east on Park Road 1, when oaks begin to dominate the landscape.

Because of the popularity of these parks, two other state parks are under construction nearby. Located on the north and south shores of Lake Bastrop, these new facilities will bring attendance in this area to

1.5 million annually. The south shore development will be completed and open as a state park first.

But the popularity of these parks has not infringed on the small town atmosphere of Bastrop. With a population of just 4,000 within the city limits and 20,000 in the community, this historic town holds onto its small town roots.

Bastrop dates back to 1829, the first in Stephen F. Austin's "little colony," located where the Camino Real crossed the Colorado River. It was named after the Baron of Bastrop, a friend of Austin's. The town grew, but sadly most of its early structures were lost in a massive fire in 1862. The downtown was rebuilt with Victorian structures, and today 130 of those historic buildings remain, including 31 Texas Medallion homes.

Stop by the **Bastrop Chamber of Commerce** (927 Main St.) for a copy of "A Walking Tour of Historic Bastrop." The tour takes you past the 1883 Courthouse, the Old Colorado River Bridge, and many downtown businesses and homes. If you're not in the mood for walking, make it a cycling tour: the Chamber rents bicycles so you can pedal through these quiet neighborhoods. Or hop aboard an elegant carriage! **Classic Carriages of Bastrop** (512-321-6351) operates from the corner of Pine and Main Streets on Friday and Saturday nights. Clip-clop through the streets past some historic structures that have witnessed the comings and goings in Bastrop since the Civil War days.

One notable downtown building is the **Bastrop Opera House** (711 Spring St., 512-321-6286), built in 1889. After a major renovation in 1978, this building is once again the cultural center of town, with live theater ranging from mysteries to vaudeville.

The downtown is also home to many antiques and specialty shops. Stop by the **1010 Gallery** (1010 Main St., 512-303-1010) for a look at artwork by talented Texas and Southwest painters and sculptors.

Whether you explore Bastrop by foot, pedal, or horse power, you'll find that this town in the pines is an ideal getaway.

F Y I 〰

Getting There: Bastrop is located southeast of Austin on TX 71.

Love Nests: Bastrop has accommodations both for those looking for a rustic hideaway or a Victorian plushness. We stayed at the Bastrop State

Park cabins, some of the most sought-after accommodations in Texas. Constructed by CCC workers, the cabins each provide all the comforts of home, from linens to kitchenettes, plus many offer fireplaces as well. Our cabin (we fondly refer to it as "our cabin" whenever we drive through the park) featured a stone fireplace with a hand-carved mantel, two bedrooms, a kitchen, a living area, and an outdoor patio with a picnic table overlooking the lake. For cabin reservations, call (512) 389-8900.

If you're looking for more historic luxury, consider a stay in one of the town's bed-and-breakfast accommodations. The Pfeiffer House (1802 Main St., 512-321-2100; $, no ☐), built in 1901, is a Victorian home with three upstairs bedrooms decorated in antique furnishings. Owner Marilyn Whites serves a full breakfast to lucky guests. Also downtown, The Colony (703 Main St., 512-303-1234; $, no ☐) treats guests with champagne and a full breakfast.

For More Information: Contact the Bastrop Chamber of Commerce (512-321-2419) for brochures on lodging, shopping, or historic attractions. For reservations at Bastrop State Park, call (512) 389-8900.

ROCKWALL
Recommended for: lake getaway, weddings

If you're looking for a place to get married, there's no more logical place than the town nicknamed "The Marrying Capital of Texas." For years Rockwall boasted the largest number of weddings in the entire Lone Star State.

It's appropriate, then, that this small town 22 miles northeast of Dallas is home to **The Wedding Cottage** (730 S. Goliad, 214-771-2340), which does 350 weddings a year. Beneath a Victorian arbor dotted with flowers, greenery, and romantic lighting, couples exchange their vows in front of a 25-foot altar of columns and arches. Groups as large as 150 guests can be accommodated, or, for intimate ceremonies, just the bride and groom. After vows are exchanged, the reception area has seating and room for dancing. With the "dream package," guests shower the newlyweds with birdseed as they depart in a white limousine to any destination in the Dallas metroplex.

Rockwall is a romantic community located on the shores of **Lake Ray Hubbard.** Considered one of the world's top inland sailing lakes, this lake has 100 miles of shoreline. Two yacht clubs, marinas, and docks give the community a marine atmosphere where guests enjoy sailing, windsurfing, fishing, and surfing.

Rockwall's history goes back far before its time as a place to get married or enjoy a weekend at the lake. The site was orginally inhabited by the Caddo Indians, then later by pioneer farmers. These early settlers tilled up the remains of an underground wall that may have been created by prehistoric man or by the upheaval of the Balcones Fault. The wall gave those founders a name for their community.

Today on the **historic square** you can still view a portion of that early "rock wall." But the ancient stones are just one reason to visit the downtown area. Here you'll also find antique shops, art galleries, and crafts stores.

As the day draws to a close, head off to the ***Texas Queen*** (Dalrock Rd. exit south off I-30 E., 214-771-0039; admission fee) for a ride aboard a 105-foot paddle wheeler. Musical entertainment keeps the spirit lively on dinner cruises scheduled Wednesday through Friday and Sunday. The double-deck boat departs from Elgin B. Robertson Park; reservations are required.

F Y I

Getting There: Rockwall is located just off I-30 northeast of Dallas.

For More Information: Call Rockwall Area Chamber of Commerce at (214) 771-5733.

COMFORT
Recommended for: antiques shopping, B&B, history

Ready to relax? Then think "gemuetlichkeit." Or just think Comfort. Northwest of San Antonio on I-10, Comfort is a community with strong German roots and ties to earlier generations. Settlers first planned to name the town "Gemuetlichkeit," meaning peace, serenity, comfort, and happiness. Fortunately, they settled on the easier-to-pronounce "Comfort."

Today "comfort" perfectly describes the atmosphere of this Hill Country community. The streets here are as busy today as they were a century ago, when customers would come in to the local establishments for kerosene, oil, and washboards. The only difference is that many of these historic structures today house antique shops, restaurants, and bed-and-breakfast inns instead of feed,

dry goods, and grocery stores of a century past. The downtown historic district boasts 120 buildings. One of Texas's oldest general stores, the **1880 Ingenhuett Store** (830 High St., 210-995-2149), is still open for business, featuring a collection of historic photos of Comfort's early days.

Other popular shopping spots include **The Comfort Common** (818 High St., 210-995-3030). Wander among the historic buildings to find the town's largest collection of antiques including primitives and furniture. Antique lovers should also stop by **Marketplatz** (7th and Main Sts., 210-995-2000). This large store offers two floors of furniture, collectibles, quilts, and crafts, all housed in an 1883 building.

One of Comfort's most unusual structures is a mile out of town on FM 473. A **bat roost,** built in 1918, was constructed here in an attempt to control malaria. The roosts were intended to encourage the area's large bat population to remain in the region and feed on disease-spreading mosquitoes. Sixteen such roosts were built in the country, and this is the oldest of the three still known to exist. The bat roost is located on private land, but visitors can pull off the road and read the historic marker located behind private gates.

If you're a bat lover, stop by the **Bat Tunnel** (15 miles northeast of Comfort off TX 473 on old Hwy. 9, 210-995-3131; free). From May until October, view the evening flight of 1.2 million Mexican free-tailed bats from this abandoned railroad tunnel now managed by the Texas Parks and Wildlife Department.

Although today the atmosphere defines Comfort, at one time things were far from comfortable. This town suffered a massacre of many of its citizens, an event called "the blackest day in the history of the Civil War."

Comfort was first settled in 1854 by German immigrants who were followers of the "Freethinker" philosophy. These settlers felt an intense loyalty to their new country and its commitment to democracy and freedom of religion. Things went well in the new land until the Civil War broke out, and Texas began to talk of seceding from the Union. The German immigrants strongly opposed secession, and some farmers openly backed the Union government, an act that the Confederates considered treasonous. Finally martial law was declared, and the Texas Rangers were sent to order all males over 16 to take an oath of allegiance to the Confederacy. When many refused, farms and homes were burned, and some dissidents were lynched. Some accounts say as many as 150 citizens were killed.

With these mounting troubles and threats to their families, a group of Comfort men decided to leave Texas and head to Mexico to wait out the war. A band of 60 left on August 1, 1862. They did not know that the Confederates had been told of their move by an informant. The Unionists were followed to the banks of the Nueces River before the attack began. When it was over, 19 Comfort citizens had been killed in battle. Nine others were captured, but they were later executed by the leader of the Confederates. Later, eight other Unionists were killed while crossing the Rio Grande near the Devil's River, their bodies left unburied until the end of the war.

It wasn't until three years later that the remains were returned and buried in a mass grave in Comfort. The next year, on August 10, 1866, the first monument in Texas was erected at the gravesite to remember this grim battle. The **Treue der Union** (or "True to the Union") **Monument** (High St. between 3rd and 4th Sts.; free) was a simple obelisk, inscribed with the names of the men who were killed. Outside of national cemeteries, this remains the only monument to the Union erected in a state south of the Mason-Dixon line.

This monument, listed in the National Register of Historic Places, is also noteworthy for another unusual feature. In 1991, the Treue der Union Monument became one of only five sites in the nation where the flag is allowed to be flown at half staff at all times. The flag flown here is the 36-star American flag, the one flown at the dedication of the monument over 125 years ago.

F Y I ⤿

Getting There: Comfort is located 52 miles northwest of San Antonio on I-10.

Nearby Attractions: In the tiny community of Sisterdale, visit Sister Creek Vineyards (FM 1376 off FM 473, 210-324-6704). This winery thrives in a restored cotton gin and produces traditional French wines. On weekdays, stop by for an afternoon tour.

Love Nests: Just down the street from the general store, the Ingenhuett family once owned the Ingenhuett-Faust Hotel. Today that historic building is the Comfort Common (818 High St., 210-995-3030; $, □), a combination bed-and-breakfast inn and antique cooperative. Travelers watch small town life from rocking chairs on the wide porches of the two-story inn. Day visitors can shop for antiques in the hotel and in several outbuildings located in the shady backyard.

For More Information: Write the Comfort Chamber of Commerce at P.O. Box 777, Comfort, TX 78013, or call (210) 995-3131.

JOHNSON CITY
Recommended for: shopping, B&Bs, history

If you're looking for a day of history and heritage that won't include museum admission costs and tour fees, then head west to Johnson City. This is the land that President Lyndon Baines Johnson called home, just as his ancestors had years before when Texas was first being settled. Today it's a small town getaway for couples seeking a little shopping and a lot of history.

Start your visit in downtown Johnson City at the **LBJ National Historic Park** (US 290 and 9th St., 210-868-7128; free). Stop by the new Visitors Center for brochures and a look at some exhibits on the late president's family, then walk to two historic areas.

From 1913 to 1934 Lyndon Johnson lived in a simple white frame house at this location. Johnson's father, Sam Ealy Johnson, Jr., was a state representative, and the home often echoed with political debate. At the same time, a future statesman was being tutored on the front porch at the knee of his mother, Rebekah Baines Johnson.

After your tour, head toward the **Johnson Settlement,** a restoration of the cabin and buildings which belonged to Sam Ealy Johnson, Sr., LBJ's grandfather. The Settlement can be reached on a path from the boyhood home, a walk through pastures which were once the Johnson's livelihood.

Photos, farm implements, and clothing from the 1800s are displayed in a visitors center. An old cypress cistern serves as a mini-auditorium in which you may hear recorded readings of letters the original settlers wrote about this rugged land. Past the center is the Sam Johnson cabin, which also served as headquarters for his longhorn drives up the Chisholm Trail. Several head of longhorn graze in the pasture, just as they have for generations. At one point, this cabin also functioned as aid station for the wounded following the Deer Creek Indian Battle.

Once you've seen all of Johnson Settlement, it's just a short drive to the **LBJ National and State Historical Parks** (west of Johnson City on US 290, 210-644-2252; free). Leave Johnson City on US 290 to Stonewall, then turn on Ranch Road 1 to the park entrance. When LBJ was alive, much of this area comprised his private ranch. Security was very tight, and Secret Service men guarded the grounds.

Today, however, the National Park Service conducts tours of the LBJ ranch. Your visit to the park begins at the visitors center, a building of native rock constructed in a typical Texas style. Displays of LBJ's family, the ranch, and the Hill Country can show you what life was like during the pioneer times, as well as the hectic days when LBJ was president. A short walk away from the building are pens of huge buffalo, native white-tailed deer, and wild turkeys.

While you're in the visitors center, sign up for a tour (admission fee) of the ranch. An air-conditioned bus with a guide will take you on a 90-minute drive around the ranch and the back pastures. The route leads you across the mighty **Pedernales River,** through a countryside dotted with cattle, live oaks, and the beauty of the Hill Country at its best. This is the land that LBJ loved and returned to as often as possible. Often during the tour, the words of LBJ and Lady Bird are broadcast over the bus's loudspeaker describing their feelings for the area.

Immediately after crossing the Pedernales River, your tour bus will slow down for photographs of the one-room schoolhouse where LBJ began his education at the age of four. A few minutes later, you'll stop at a recreation of the home where LBJ was born. Built in a breezy style typical of Texas homes of the period, the house is filled with furnishings of the Johnsons. Before heading back to the bus, stop by the family cemetery nearby. It lies under the shade of huge oak trees and overlooks the Pedernales River. LBJ and many members of his family are buried here.

Your tour continues with a drive past the **"Texas White House,"** a large white home sprawled under shady oaks. Many national and international names visited this Texas White House during LBJ's lifetime.

For the remainder of the tour, you'll see just what ranch life is like in Central Texas. Cattle graze lazily over the many pastures; ranch hands cut hay; workers clean the stockbarn used for cattle sales. This is still very much a working ranch.

Although the LBJ sites can easily fill a day, you'll find plenty of other diversions in Johnson City. Shop at **The Feed Mill** (US 290, 210-868-7299), a new complex that utilizes a former feed mill and transforms it into a compendium of shopping and dining opportunities. You don't need an address to find this shopping mall—just look for most unusual building in town. Antique and import stores, a wine tasting and retail store, an art gallery, and other small specialty stores are scattered through the complex, which is decorated in a surrealistic style with everything from armadillos to zebras to farm tools.

Just across the road, **Horse Feathers Mall** (US 290 and Ave. F, 210-868-4147) combines antiques, woodwork, leather goods, and collectibles in both open-air and enclosed spaces.

F Y I ❧

Getting There: Johnson City is located in the Hill Country on US 290.

Dining: There's one restaurant in Johnson City that has received nationwide attention: Uncle Kunkel's Bar B Q (208 US 281 S., 210-868-7074; $, ☐). For years the Kunkels did the catering for the LBJ Ranch, and today they prepare their award-winning pork ribs, brisket, and sausage for the public. Have a plate of smoked meats with side dishes of potato salad, coleslaw, or pinto beans, followed by a slice of homemade pie.

Love Nests: Choose from seven properties of Bed and Breakfast of Johnson City (210-868-4548; $–$$; ☐), including the Hill House Guest

House. One of the city's oldest homes, it was built at the turn of the century and modernized with a tin exterior in the 1920s. This bed-and-breakfast has been used by many wedding parties and anniversary couples, and recently a newlywed couple in their 90s. Other accommodations include the Lawyer's Loft (with hand-carved mahogany beds), Smith's Tin House on the Square (a two-bedroom cottage), Boot Hill Guest House (decorated with items straight out of the Old West), Hoppe's Guest House (a private guest house served by the owners located next door), the Gingerbread House (a two-bedroom cottage with kitchen), and Carolyne's Cottage (owned by a certified massage therapist who can provide relaxing treatments). Each of these homes is a guest house, not a traditional bed-and-breakfast, so couples do enjoy complete privacy.

For More Information: Contact the Johnson City Chamber of Commerce at (210) 868-7684.

LA GRANGE
Recommended for: history, small town charm

Folks from around the world think of La Grange as home of "The Best Little Whorehouse in Texas." The memory of the **Chicken Ranch** lives on, although the country's most famous brothel is long gone. But Central Texans have a different view of La Grange. To locals, it's a quiet farm town with a classic Texas courthouse square. It's a barbecue hotspot, a place to enjoy smoky

beef brisket and tender ribs served on butcher paper. It's the home of a historic park where you can take the family and experience a quiet nature walk.

The county seat of Fayette County, La Grange is located southeast of Austin on TX 71 at the spot where an old trail called La Bahia Road crossed the Colorado River. Founded by settlers from Fayette County,

Kentucky, in 1831, the town was christened after La Grange, Tennessee. For years, the town carried on quietly in the middle of this rolling farming region.

Since the demise of the Chicken Ranch, La Grange's best known attraction is **Monument Hill State Park** (1 mile south of town on US 77, 409-968-5658; admission fee), perched atop a bluff overlooking the Colorado River. You'll reach the park by driving to the region's highest point. From this hilltop, visitors have a spectacular view of La Grange and the surrounding farmlands that spread out for miles.

Monument Hill is a quiet place, fitting for a memorial of two tragic events in Texas history. This is the burial place for the Texans who died in the **Dawson Massacre** and the **Mier Expedition,** two historic conflicts that occurred in 1842, six years after fall of the Alamo. The Dawson Massacre took place near San Antonio when La Grange citizen Nicholas Dawson gathered Texans to combat the continued attacks by the Mexican army. Dawson's men were met by hundreds of Mexican troops and 35 Texans were killed.

The Mexican village of Mier was attacked in a retaliatory move, resulting in the capture of Texas soldiers and citizens by Mexican General Santa Anna, who ordered every tenth man to be killed. The Texans were blindfolded and forced to draw beans—159 of them white and 17 black. Men who drew white beans were imprisoned; those who drew black ones were executed.

The bodies of the Texans were returned here to be buried on the hilltop in a mass grave. Nearly a century later in 1936 the state erected a tall monument to honor these fallen Texans. Today the entire hilltop, a spot once known as "The Bluffs," is a state park. You'll find a visitors center here explaining the confrontations.

The park also remembers a far happier time in Texas history, the founding of one of Texas's first breweries. **Kreische Brewery** was started here by German immigrant Heinreich Kreische in 1849. The brewmaster purchased the hilltop and the adjoining land, including the burial ground of those Texas heroes, for his brewery site. Eventually he became the third largest beer producer in the state. The kettles are long gone now, but you can take a guided tour of the ruins on weekends. The tour takes you past the two-story house that was once home to Kreische and his family and to the brewery site. Today the brewery is reduced to ruins, the remnants of a few limestone walls, the only reminders of Heinreich Kreische's hard work.

The brewery tour is included in the entrance fee for Monument Hill. Although you can walk through the brewery remains only during weekend guided tours, you can take the nature walk to view the site any time.

During his day, Heinrich Kreische probably picked up some pharmaceutical items at **Hermes Drug Store** (148 N. Washington St., 409-968-5835) in La Grange. Even today you can run by for a bottle of aspirin or a box of bandages because Hermes is still in business and holds the title as the oldest drugstore in continuous operation in Texas.

While you're downtown, pick up some barbecue for lunch on the square at **Prause's Barbecue** (US 77 on the square, 409-968-3259; $, no ☐). This meat market serves up smoky delights on butcher-paper plates. Get there early on weekends; Prause's closes when the food runs out. And don't bother to come by on Sundays; that's when the "Gone Fishing" sign is out.

Another local favorite is **Prime Bar-B-Q** (Hwy. 159 and 71 Bypass Feeder Rd., 409-968-8033; $, no ☐). This no-nonsense place serves pork ribs, sausage, chicken, and plenty of beef brisket with side dishes of baked potato salad, coleslaw, and pinto beans, followed by a dip of banana pudding.

La Grange is also home to another famous eatery, the **Bon Ton Restaurant** (TX 71 west of town, 409-968-5863; $, ☐). This combination restaurant and bakery is always busy with locals and travelers who have heard of the Bon Ton's reputation for good home cooking. Daily specials and a popular buffet tempt diners with chicken-fried steak, fried chicken, mashed potatoes, fried okra, and fresh rolls. Don't miss the homemade *kolaches* and bread.

F Y I ✎

Getting There: La Grange is between Austin and Houston on TX 71.

Festivals/Special Events: For old-fashioned, small town fun, including a carnival, stock show, and plenty of food, visit La Grange during the Fayette County Fair. One of the biggest events of the year, the fair is held on Labor Day weekend at the Fayette County Fairgrounds.

For More Information: Call the La Grange Chamber of Commerce at (409) 968-5756.

CASTROVILLE
Recommended for: B&Bs, antique shopping, fine dining

Imagine a place where the 19th and 20th centuries join together, treating visitors to modern conveniences and comforts in an Old World atmosphere. Add to this a gazpacho of cultures, a blend of French, German, English, and Spanish with a heavy dose of Alsatian heritage. What you get is Castroville, located 20 miles west of San Antonio. This town, nicknamed "The Little Alsace of Texas," may be near the Alamo City, but in terms of mood and atmosphere it's in another world.

If you want a taste of the Old World—while leaving your passport at home—then Castroville's the place. Here, amid historic structures built in the European tradition, you can shop for antiques, dine on fine Alsatian food, and then end the day in a B&B filled with antique furnishings.

Castroville's emphasis on history and its Old World roots is an honest one. The community was founded by Frenchman Henri Castro, who contracted with the Republic of Texas to bring settlers from Europe. These pioneers came from the French province of Alsace in 1844, bringing with them the Alsatian language, a Germanic dialect. Today only the oldest residents of Castroville carry on the mother tongue.

Traditional Alsatian houses sport European-style, nonsymmetrical, steeply sloping roofs. To have a look at this distinctive architecture, take a self-guided tour of **Old Castroville.** Pick up a free map from the **Castroville Chamber of Commerce** (802 London St.). This town boasts 97 historic homes and buildings, including Henri Castro's homestead, a 1910 meat market, an 1854 gristmill, and homes dating back to the earliest pioneers. The entire section known as Old Castroville is now a National Historic District.

With Castroville's rich history, it's not surprising that the community is a magnet for antique dealers. Fifteen antique shops dot the downtown area. Park and walk the historic streets with names like Paris, London, Madrid, and Petersburg where you'll find shops offering furniture, glassware, china, pottery, and collectibles of all kinds.

Castroville is unique because it boasts two town squares. **Houston Square** is the original town square, located in front of the **St. Louis**

Church in Old Castroville. **September Square** sits across the Medina River bridge, commemorating the arrival of those first pioneers on September 4, 1844. September Square is also the home of the **Landmark Inn.**

Whether you want to shop, tour, or dine, the local residents have one bit of Alsatian advice: "Kum sah Castroville!" ("Come see Castroville!")

F Y I ❧

Getting There: Castroville is located 20 miles west of San Antonio on US 90.

Festivals/Special Events: Castroville hosts many special events through the year. During the last weekend in September and the third weekend in May, over 75 antique dealers from around the country come to town for an antique show. Shoppers should also mark on their calendars the second Saturday from March through December, when Castroville hosts the Market Trail Days, a shopping extravaganza with everything from arts and crafts to antiques to food.

Dining: One of the most popular local restaurants is The Alsatian (403 Angelo St., 210-931-3260; $$, ☐), open daily for lunch and Thursday through Sunday for dinner. Housed in a historic 19th-century cottage typical of the provincial homes of Castroville, this restaurant specializes in Alsatian and German food, including spicy Alsatian sausage, *jagerschnitzel,* and German-style pork chops. For something lighter, try Haby's Alsatian Bakery (207 US 290 E., 210-931-2118; $, no ☐). Try to choose from among apple strudel, molasses cookies, and fresh baked breads.

Love Nests: Perhaps the best way to absorb the atmosphere of Castroville is with a stay in one of its bed-and-breakfast inns. The most famous is the Landmark Inn (402 Florence St., 512-389-8900; $, no ☐), operated by the Texas Parks and Wildlife Department. This inn was first a home and general store before becoming the Vance Hotel. Robert E. Lee and Bigfoot Wallace, the famous Texas Ranger, were said to have stayed at the hotel that was renamed the Landmark Inn during World War II.

Today's guests select from eight historic rooms decorated with antique furnishings. The absence of telephones and televisions helps transport visitors back to the previous century, when visitors to the hotel enjoyed a welcome rest from the stagecoaches traveling the Old San Antonio–El Paso Road. During warmer months, six of the eight rooms are air-conditioned, and all include heaters. Guests enjoy a continental breakfast served in the 1849 kitchen.

Even if you don't have the pleasure of staying overnight in one of the eight historic rooms, stop by the inn for a look at the museum containing displays illustrating Henri Castro's early efforts to recruit settlers, as well as exhibits covering early Castroville life. You can also enjoy a self-guided tour of the beautifully manicured inn grounds and have a look at the 1850s grist mill and dam and the old bathhouse.

Visitors can also call Castroville's First Bed and Breakfast Registry (800-329-9622) for information on accommodations.

For More Information: Contact the Chamber of Commerce at P.O. Box 572, Castroville, TX 78009, or call (210) 538-3142.

TYLER
Recommended for: rose lovers, B&Bs

There's not a Texas city with a rosier future—or a past—than Tyler. This community of 75,000 is the "City of Roses," known throughout the rose world for its beautiful blooms. Tyler roses are shipped all over the country and to 25 foreign nations.

From May through November, the flower of lovers is at its peak throughout the city, especially at the **Tyler Municipal Rose Garden** (W. Front St. at Rose Park Dr., 903-531-1212; free). Here 22 acres bloom with 38,000 rose bushes that fill the air with a heavenly scent. For information on roses, the area's rose-growing industry, and October's popular Rose Festival, including queens' dresses, visit the museum.

Continue your look at Tyler with a stop at some of its leading attractions, including the **Tyler Museum of Art** (1300 S. Mahon Ave., 903-595-1001; free). This museum, adjacent to the Tyler Junior College, features changing exhibits usually devoted to one artist.

Also at Tyler Junior College you can tour one of Texas's largest planetariums, the **Hudnall Planetarium** (off TX 64 at the college, 903-510-2312; admission fee). Along with displays of replicas of exploratory space vehicles, the planetarium also offers regularly scheduled shows on Wednesday and Sunday afternoons (as well as private shows on other days; call for availability). Occasional star parties are often scheduled. Free of charge, these parties give you the opportunity to use high-powered telescopes and view the heavens above East Texas.

That East Texas setting that surrounds Tyler is one of its most treasured attractions, and you can enjoy the piney forests at **Tyler State Park** (10 miles north on FM 14 and Park Rd. 16, 903-597-5338; admission fee). This 994-acre park is considered one of the most beautiful forest areas in the state and can be appreciated by campers, picknickers, hikers, and fishermen.

F Y I ≈

Getting There: Tyler is located in East Texas on I-20 and US 69.

Nearby Attractions: Save time for a ride on the Texas State Railroad, a true "iron horse" than travels 50 miles roundtrip between Rusk and Palestine. The route winds through piney woods, across 30 bridges, and into depots built to recall the heyday of steam-powered travel. In Rusk, a small theater shows a film on the history of the railroad.

The peak time for travel on this popular train is spring, when flowering dogwood trees dot the landscape. Any time of year, however, reservations are recommended. In Texas, call (800) 442-8951; outside the state call (903) 683-2561 to reserve two seats on this romantic ride.

Festivals/Special Events: Tyler's festivals are bloomin' good. In March, the Azalea and Spring Flower Trail follows seven miles of home gardens along with special events such as a chili cook-off, a quilt show, a blues festival, and heritage home tours. For information, call (903) 592-1661.

In late October, the Texas Rose Festival celebrates the fall blooms as it has for over six decades. Events include the Rose Show, Rose Queen's Coronation, Rose Parade, rose field tours, arts and crafts fair, dance, and more.

Shopping: Tyler is often used as a home base for shoppers in nearby Canton during First Mondays Trade Days (see "Canton" in the "Shop 'til You (Both) Drop" chapter of this book).

Love Nests: Tyler is home to two neighboring bed-and-breakfast homes that offer traditional elegance. Located between the historic district and the azalea district, the stately homes are favorite stops for romantically minded travelers and for wedding parties.

Charnwood Hill (223 E. Charnwood Rd., 903-597-3980; $-$$$, ☐) was once the home of Texas's well-known Hunt family. The millionaire family spared no expense in their palatial home; this is, without a doubt, one of Texas's finest B&Bs. Now owned by the Walker family, they've converted the elegant home into a B&B that makes every guest fill like a millionaire. The home drips with elegance, from its crystal chandeliers to its Oriental rugs to its fine antiques. Guests can choose from five double rooms and a suite.

Just next door stands Tyler's newest B&B, The Seasons (313 E. Charnwood Rd., 903-533-0803; $-$$, ☐). This 1911 home has been transformed into a work of art by owner Myra Brown, an artist specializing in wallscapes. Myra has brought her skills to this home, transforming each of the four guest rooms into a representation of the season for which it is named. The Summer Room comes alive with geraniums, the Fall Room is crisp with rag-rolled walls done in an autumnal shade, and the Winter Room recreates a Victorian ice-skating park, complete with small park benches and white sheepskin rugs in front of a fireplace, with a painted backdrop of skaters on an outdoor pond. Our favorite was the Spring Room, with sunny corner windows, a picket fence bed, a painted arbor on the walls, and furnishings that carry on the theme of the Secret Garden.

For More Information: Call the Tyler Area Convention and Visitors at (800) 235-5712.

GOD'S IN HIS HEAVEN—ALL'S RIGHT WITH THE WORLD!

FORGOTTEN
GETAWAYS

REMEMBER, ROMANCE, LIKE BEAUTY, IS IN the eye of the beholder. Enter a getaway with an open mind, and you'll find that many cities you may have written off as "unromantic" can bring a real twinkle to your eye.

These communities aren't often considered lovers' retreats, but each offers good attractions for couples, from Texas's largest canyon where you can enjoy a technicolor sunset to a museum featuring the belongings of Robert and Elizabeth Browning to concert halls offering live musical entertainment. Grab your partner and two-step over to these cities for a romantic getaway weekend.

TEXARKANA
Recommended for: B&Bs, museums, opera, theater

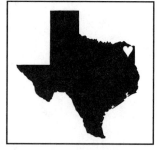

On the very edge of Texas where the Lone Star State meets Arkansas lies Texarkana, a city of 60,000 residents that strides the state line. This site had been a point in a trail between Indian villages; in the mid-1800s it saw a new transportation line—the railroad.

The significance of the railroad industry is still felt in Texarkana today. Visit **Union Station** (Front St.), which can be entered from either Texas or Arkansas. The station once saw as many as 20 trains a day; today the activity focuses in its restaurant and meeting rooms.

That state line has also created a somewhat unusual tourist stop: the **Post Office** (State Line Ave.). The only U.S. Post Office located in two states, you can enter it from either one. Step outside to **Photographer's Island** (State Line Ave.) for the requisite shot of your traveling companion standing with one foot in each state.

History lovers will find plenty to keep them happy in this city. Just a few blocks from the Post Office lies the unusual **Ace of Clubs House** (420 Pine St., 903-793-7108; admission fee). This is a true house of cards. Built in 1885 in Italianate Victorian style, the 22-sided grand manse is built in the shape of an ace of clubs. Word around town is that the house's owner, James H. Draughton, built the mansion with his winnings from a poker game. Today visitors can take a guided tour of about an hour for a look at the palatial home, its central octagonal hallway, and its three octagonal wings.

Arts—both visual and performing—play an important role in Texarkana. The **Regional Arts Center** (321 W. 4th St., 903-792-8681; admission fee) was originally constructed in 1909 as a U.S. District Courthouse. Today judgment is passed on its displays: works of nationally touring juried and invitational exhibitions. The building has recently been restored to its turn-of-the-century grandeur, including a grand hall with a 26-foot-high ceiling.

Texarkana's most noted historic figure was ragtime musician Scott Joplin. Born in the stateline city on November 24, 1868, Joplin grew up here before heading off to St. Louis as a young man. Today Joplin's accomplishments are remembered with displays at the **Texarakana Historical Museum** (219 State Ave., 903-793-4831; small admission fee) and **Discovery Place** (Pine St., 903-794-3466; admission fee). You can also view the **Scott Joplin Mural** (3rd and Main Sts.; free), an outdoor mural that outlines the accomplishments of the Pulitzer Prize–winning composer. Commissioned by the Texarkana Regional Arts and Humanities Council, the colorful scene keeps alive the memory of the "King of Ragtime Composers."

Texarkana's other native son is H. Ross Perot. The billionaire has restored a 1924 theater and brought world-class performances to Texarkana at the **Perot Theatre** (219 Main St., 800-333-0927 for tickets, 903-792-8681 for a tour). For many couples, this grand theater is reason enough to visit Texarkana. From September through May, the Perot Series brings major symphony orchestras, classical ballet, Broadway productions, and popular performers from the worlds of pop and country music to this community.

F Y I

Getting There: Texarkana is located on the Arkansas-Texas border on I-30.

Festivals/Special Events: For 10 days in mid-September, Texarkana puts on its 10-gallon hat and boots and gets ready for the Four States Fair and Rodeo. This gala features a PRCA Rodeo, carnival, and horseshow. For information, call (501) 773-2941.

Dining: For a true Texas steak, head to the Cattleman's Steak House (4018 State Line Ave., 501-774-4481; $$–$$$, □). The menu also features barbecue ribs, seafood, and prime rib.

Looking for French cuisine? Try Park Place (2905 Arkansas Blvd., 501-772-2201; $$, □). Along with fine French dishes, they also offer up prime rib and seafood in an elegant atmosphere.

For a taste of New Orleans, check out The Faded Rose (215 Walnut St., 501-779-1215; $$–$$$, □). Treat your taste buds to red beans and rice, gumbo, New Orleans–style steaks, seafood, and more in this casual restaurant.

Love Nests: Texarkana also has another good reason to visit: Mansion on the Main (802 Main St., 903-792-1835; $, □). Tom and Peggy Taylor, the owners of Jefferson's McKay House (see the "Jefferson" section in "Bed-and-Breakfast Getaways") also own this Neoclassical B&B built in 1895. Guests can choose from five double rooms with baths and one suite, all decorated with period antiques. For fun, Peggy has period hats available for guests to wear to breakfast.

For More Information: Call the Texarkana Chamber of Commerce at (903) 792-7191. While in Texarkana, stop by the Texas Tourist Information Center (just over the Texas state line on I-30) for brochures and maps for the Texarkana area and for all of Texas.

ARLINGTON
Recommended for: live shows, shopping, dining

Our memories of Arlington go back to our childhood days. After all, this is the hometown of Six Flags Over Texas, the equivalent of mecca for young Texans. Later, we knew Arlington as the home of the Texas Rangers baseball team. In recent years, we watched the home team move into the new ballpark in Arlington, constructed to recall the nostalgic days of the sport.

But we've also learned to appreciate Arlington as a couple as well. Often overlooked except as a family destination, we found that this city has plenty of thrills outside its roller-coaster rides to keep a couple happy for the weekend.

Live entertainment is becoming increasingly popular in this Dallas–Fort Worth Metroplex city. **Johnnie High's Country Music Revue** (Arlington Music Hall, 224 N. Center St., 800-540-5127; admission fee) offers variety shows à la Branson, Missouri, every Saturday in both matinee and evening performances. A gospel show is also offered on Friday nights. The 1,200-seat theater is usually a sell-out; crowds enjoy the country and 50s rock 'n' roll of the live show.

Theatre Arlington (305 W. Main St., 817-275-7661; admission fee) is another popular venue for couples. For nearly 25 years the theater has offered productions such as *Cabaret, Hair!, Vanities,* and *Joseph* *and the Amazing Technicolor Dreamcoat.* Lobby bistro tables are popular with couples before the show and at intermission; enjoy a glass of wine as you talk about the production. Shows are held Thursday through Saturday evenings.

F Y I 〜

Getting There: Arlington is tucked between Dallas and Fort Worth on I-30.

Nearby Attractions: If you're a dedicated bargain hunter, make a stop by Traders Village, located in the nearby city of Grand Prairie. Since 1973, over 35 million people have visited this famous market, which now sprawls across 106 acres.

Traders Village combines equal parts of garage sale, antique shop, and carnival. "This is a little city on weekends," points out Ron Simmons, president of the flea market. "On a good weekend, we'll have anywhere from 50,000 to 80,000 people and 1,400 to 1,600 vendors. We have everything new and used under the sun."

And so they do. We found antique farm implements, quilts, vintage clothing, Raggedy Ann dolls, marbles, and china sold alongside new gardening gloves, sunglasses, and sweatshirts. Hunting among the garage sale booths is like looking for buried treasure. With enough patience and a good eye, any kind of bargain was possible.

When Trader's Village began in the early '70s, this part of Grand Prairie was just a cotton field on the Texas plains. To lure customers to the flea market, the owners devised a series of special events. Today the flea market would do just fine without these celebrations, but no one would dream of stopping the fun.

Special events stretch throughout the year and, just like it is to the flea market, admission is free. In June, the village hosts the antique auto swap meet. Other events throughout the year include a barbecue cook-off, Oktoberfest, an annual prairie dog chili cook-off, the World Championship of Pickled Quail Egg Eating (really), and, the best known and most colorful event, the National Championship Indian Pow-Wow in September.

The flea market is open every Saturday and Sunday, year-round, from 8 a.m. to dusk. Admission is always free, and parking is just a couple of bucks. Trader's Village is located at 2602 Mayfield Road in Grand

Prairie, just five miles south of Six Flags Over Texas theme park off TX 360. For more information, call (214) 647-2331.

Festivals/Special Events: December is Arlington's most festive month. On the first weekend, visit the Feast of Carols Renaissance Festival (University of Texas at Arlington, 817-273-2962; admission fee) for an evening of feasting, songs, and performance. Also in December, visit the Interlochen Lights (West Arlington at Randol Mill and Meadowbrook, 800-433-5374; free). This neighborhood is illuminated by thousands of lights and probably an equal number of visitors who come to slowly drive through the region and appreciate the Christmas cheer of the Lake Arlington neighborhood. Also in December, Six Flags celebrates with Holiday in the Park (Six Flags Over Texas, 817-640-8900; admission fee). The 200-acre park is filled with lights and decorations, and visitors can enjoy a Christmas musical, a ride down Snow Hill (thanks to snow-making equipment), and an evening parade.

Dining: Itself a destination is Cacharel Restaurant (2221 E. Lamar Blvd., 817-640-9981; $$$, □). This French restaurant has been named one of the top 50 restaurants in the country by *Conde Nast Traveler* and features an extensive wine list to accompany traditional French cuisine, exotic game, and traditional French desserts. Reservations are required.

For lunch, visit one of Arlington's tea rooms. The Rose Garden Tearoom (3708 W. Pioneer Pkwy., 817-795-3093; $–$$, □) is located in an antique mall, providing sustenance so you don't shop 'til you drop. Lunch on quiche, soup, or sandwiches. Similarly, The Tea Garden (1715 Lamar, 817-861-2760; $–$$, □) is also located in an antique mall and offers up quiche, pasta, soups, and salads accompanied by wine. Take a mid-afternoon break with English high tea from 2 to 4 p.m. for hot or cold tea, finger sandwiches, petit fours, and scones. Reservations for high tea are required.

Love Nests: Check out one of Arlington's hotel packages. The Arlington Hilton (2401 E. Lamar Blvd., 817-640-3322; $$, □) offers up a romance package with an alcove suite, breakfast, late check out, and champagne. The Radisson Suite Hotel (700 Ave. H East, 817-640-0440; $$, □) tempts visitors with packages that include champagne and strawberries, cocktails, breakfast, and a candlelight dinner in your room. Holiday Inn (1507 N. Watson Rd., 817-640-7712; $, □) treats guests to the

"Heart to Heart" package, including a king-size bed, champagne, breakfast for two, and a basket of goodies.

For More Information: Call the Arlington Convention and Visitors Bureau at (800) 433-5374. When in Arlington, drop by the Visitors Center near the Six Flags entrance at 921 Six Flags Drive for free brochures and maps.

WACO
Recommended for: museums

"How do I love thee?
Let me count the ways."

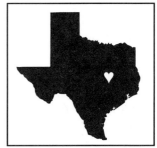

If you're a fan of the Brownings' soulful verses, then make plans to go to Waco. Few Texans would consider Waco a romantic destination, but this Central Texas city is the home of the state's most romantic museum: the **Armstrong-Browning Library** (8th and Speight Sts., 817-755-3566; free). Located on the grounds of Baylor University, this two-story museum features the works of Elizabeth Barrett Browning and husband Robert Browning. The building also boasts the world's largest collection of secular stained-glass windows, which illustrate the works of both writers (including Robert Browning's "The Pied Piper of Hamlin"). Take a guided tour to see the upstairs rooms furnished with the couple's belongings.

This city of over 100,000 is named for the Hueco (pronounced "WAY-co") Indians who resided here before the days of recorded history. The Hueco were attracted to this rich, fertile land at the confluence of the Brazos and Bosque Rivers. Although Spanish explorers named this site "Waco Village" in 1542, over 300 years elapsed before permanent settlement began. At that time, Waco was part of the Wild West, with cattle drives, cowboys, and so many gunslingers that stagecoach drivers called the town "Six-Shooter Junction." (Drivers commonly asked passengers to strap on their guns before the stagecoach reached the rowdy community!) In the late 1800s Waco became a center of trade with the completion of a 474-foot suspension bridge across the Brazos.

Some of the most scenic areas in Waco fall along the **Brazos River.** This waterway slices the city in half and provides miles of shoreline parks, shady walks, and downtown camping areas. Most interstate travelers are familiar with **Fort Fisher Park** (I-35 exit 335 B, 817-750-5996; free). This park was once the site of Fort Fisher, an outpost of the Texas Rangers built in 1837. The lawmen established a post here to protect the Brazos River crossing. Today the park contains the **City of Waco Tourist Information Center** (800-WACO-FUN), with plenty of brochures and helpful travel counselors, and a 35-acre campground with screened shelters on the riverbanks.

The park is also the home to the **Texas Rangers Hall of Fame and Museum** (Fort Fisher, 817-750-5986; admission fee). If you're interested in the taming of Texas, budget a couple of hours for this large museum. Visitors here can see guns of every description used by the Rangers, who had the reputation of lone lawmen who always got their man. Dioramas in the Hall of Fame recount the early days of the Rangers, including their founding by Stephen F. Austin. A 20-minute slide show runs on the hour. Visit the **James Michener Library,** adjacent to the circular theater, for a look at the author's personal effects.

Just behind Fort Fisher at Canal Street and University Parks Drive you can travel back in history at the **Governor Bill and Vara Daniel Historic Village** (Canal St. and University Parks Dr., 817-755-1160; admission fee). For a taste of Waco's days as "Six-Shooter Junction," visit this recreation of a 19th-century riverboat town. It contains a schoolhouse, a mercantile store, and, of course, a Wild West saloon. The buildings, once the property of Governor Daniel, were moved to this site from a plantation community in Liberty County, Texas, and restored by Baylor University.

More riverside attractions are found west of Fort Fischer at **University Parks Drive** between Franklin and Washington Streets. This is the home of the **suspension bridge** often used as a symbol of Waco. Spanning the 800-mile-long Brazos River, this restored structure was once the longest suspension bridge in the world. Built in 1870 (as designed by the same engineers who would construct New York's Brooklyn Bridge years later), it eliminated the time-consuming process of having to cart cattle across the water by ferry. Today it's used as a pedestrian bridge bearing the motto "First across, still across."

It's a short drive from the bridge to the **Dr. Pepper Museum** (300 S. 5th St., 817-757-1024; admission fee). The famous Dr. Pepper soft drink was invented by pharmacist Dr. Charles Alderton at the Old Corner Drug Store in Waco, which once stood at Fourth Street and Austin Avenue. Today the drugstore is gone, but the original bottling plant remains open as a museum. Interesting exhibits and films offer a look at some early promotional materials as well as the manufacturing process of the unusual soft drink. Don't miss the popular advertising slogan promoting Dr. Pepper as an energy booster to be consumed at "10-2-and-4." After a look through the museum, visit the recreation of the **Old Corner Drug Store** fountain for an ice cream soda or (what else?) a Dr. Pepper.

The Dr. Pepper Museum is certainly one of the most entertaining, but Waco is also the home to some serious museums as well. For fine arts, head to **The Art Center** (1300 College Dr., 817-752-4371; free). This exhibit hall and teaching center is located in the Mediterranean-style home of the late lumber magnate William Waldo Cameron. Exhibits here focus on Texas artists in all media.

Texans who wielded not a paintbrush but a baseball or football are featured at the **Texas Sports Hall of Fame** (University Parks Dr. and I-35, 817-756-1633; admission fee). Waco's newest attraction is a tribute to the athletes of the Lone Star State. Sports memorabilia highlight more than 350 sports heroes, including an autographed baseball by Texas Ranger Nolan Ryan, Earl Campbell's letter jacket, and one of Martina Navratilova's Wimbledon rackets, as well as displays featuring prominent Texas high school athletes.

Another new Waco attraction is the **Cameron Park Zoo** (N. 4th St. west of I-35, 817-750-8400; admission fee). Replacing an outdated zoo, this new attraction features natural habitats and displays including the African savanna, Gibbon Island, and Treetop Village.

F Y I ≈

Getting There: Waco is located between Dallas and Austin on I-35.

Dining: The most romantic restaurant in town is the *Brazos Queen II* (I-35 S., Fort Fisher exit, 817-757-2332; $$–$$$; □). Anchored just below the I-35 bridge, this restaurant features steaks and seafood. It's popular with locals for special occasions.

For More Information: For brochures on Waco or information on overnight accommodations, call (800) WACO-FUN.

LUBBOCK
Recommended for: winery tours, museums

Spend an afternoon touring elegant wineries. Take in rooms filled with high-tech stainless steel vats and European oak casks. Sip Chardonnay, Chenin Blanc, and Cabernet Sauvignon in a million-dollar tasting room.

A scene from California's Napa Valley? Sure. But you can have the same experience in Lubbock. Located on a plain Spanish explorer Francisco Coronado named the *Llano Estacado,* the Lubbock vineyards enjoy perfect growing conditions and soil. With an elevation of 3,400 feet, a semiarid climate, and an annual rainfall of about 18 inches, the area has proven to be ideal for this crop. Lubbock area grapes are shipped to wineries throughout Texas. And their home product has won numerous international awards and been served at state dinners to President Bush, Mikhail Gorbachev, and Queen Elizabeth.

Probably the most celebrated winery in the state is **Llano Estacado** (806-745-2258). Sold throughout the United States and in many European countries, Texas's most award-winning winery produces Cabernet Sauvignon, Merlot, Chardonnay, Chenin Blanc, Sauvignon Blanc, Johannisberg Reisling, Llano Blush, and other varieties. After a tour of the winery operations, enjoy a tasting of these fine wines.

The most beautiful winery in the Lubbock area is **Cap*Rock Winery** (806-863-2704), housed in a European-style chalet. The second largest winery in the state, the facility is 23,000 square feet. The striking buiding is a Southwestern design, with 14-foot ceilings and an elegant interior.

The fruit of the plains is just one attraction Lubbock has to offer couples, however. **The Lubbock Symphony Orchestra** (1721 Broadway, 806-794-7175) and **Ballet Lubbock** (Lubbock Civic Center Theater, 806-740-0505) each feature guest artists during their annual seasons.

At the **Godbold Cultural Center** (19th St., 806-741-1953) you can enjoy both visual and performing arts. Galleries display both locally and internationally known artists, and the Main Stage Center offers performances of ballet, classical music, jazz, and drama (mostly evenings).

Enjoy a light lunch or a cup of expresso, and even do a little shopping while you're here.

Art lovers should also save time for the **Fine Arts Center** (2600 Ave. P., 806-767-2686; free). Changing exhibitions feature artwork from photography to sculpture.

As home of Texas Tech University, this city also contains several excellent museums. The **Ranching Heritage Center** (4th and Indiana, 806-742-2482; free) is an outdoor museum featuring historic ranch homes and outbuildings that have been moved to this site to depict the history of ranching and its importance on the Panhandle plains. Also on campus, the **Moody Planetarium** (4th and Indiana, 806-742-2490; small admission fee) gives you the opportunity to see special planetarium programs.

Buddy Holly fans, take note. This is the rock 'n' roll legend's home town, and he is honored with a statue and "Walk of Fame" (8th Ave. and Ave. Q, free). Located in front of the **Lubbock Memorial Civic Center,** the bronze statue is the centerpiece of the circular walk which honors West Texas musicians.

F Y I 〰

Getting There: Lubbock is located in the Panhandle on I-27.

Nearby Attractions: South of Lubbock, the town of Post is home to Old Mill Trade Days, the area's largest antique show and flea market. Scheduled for the Friday, Saturday, and Sunday before the first Monday of each month, the sale draws as any as 500 vendors.

Festivals/Special Events: Lubbock has special events scheduled year-round, and several are of special interest to couples. In March, the Taste of Lubbock . . . A Cork and Fork Affair features over 30 restaurants and a dozen Texas wineries, with demonstrations on food preparation and live entertainment. In late April and early May, don't miss the Lubbock Arts Festival. This free festival is one of the largest art festivals in the state, showcasing both visual and performing arts.

Dining: The Warehouse District is home to many of the city's best eateries and nightspots. Our favorite is Stubb's Bar-B-Q (620 19th St., 806-747-4777; $-$$, □). Although Christopher "Stubb" Stubblefield is now gone, his legacy continues with tender brisket and ribs served up with live music on the side.

Love Nests: Located just down the street from Texas Tech University, the Broadway Manor (1811 Broadway, 806-749-4707 or 800-749-4707; $, □) was built in 1923. Today the home, once a fraternity house, has been completely restored and offers four rooms. The most unique room is The Lodge, the basement-turned-guest quarters. Caramel-colored pine walls, antlers above a rock fireplace, antique sewing tables, and a buffalo-plaid comforter give the large room, with a separate outdoor entrance, a woodsy feel.

In nearby Post, check into the Hotel Garza (302 E. Main, 806-495-3962; $, □) for a taste of the Old West. Breakfast is served in an elegant dining room that spans most of the first floor of this former railroad hotel; upstairs rooms are small and simple, complete with many original furnishings. The hotel offers packages that include accommodations and show tickets for live performances at the nearby Garza Theater.

Bridal Bits: For wedding vows toasted with local wine, check out Cap*Rock, available for weddings, luncheons, and dinners.

For More Information: Call the Lubbock Convention and Visitors Bureau at (800) 692-4035.

AMARILLO
Recommended for: hiking, picnicking, antique shopping

Want to get your kicks on Route 66? Then spend a weekend in Amarillo. The historic highway runs right through the heart of this Panhandle city, and the structures that once housed theaters, roadside cafes, and drugstores are now chock full of antique and collectibles shops, diners, and buildings that hark back to the region's heyday.

Amarillo is the cultural and commercial capital of the Texas Panhandle. From a humble beginning as a staging area for the Fort Worth and Denver City Railroad in the 1880s, the city became a center for cattle ranching, wheat and cotton farming, and oil production. Today, Amarillo is a city of 170,000 residents, home to Amarillo College, the Amarillo Symphony Orchestra, and the Lone Star Ballet.

For years, Amarillo has had a reputation as a speck on otherwise featureless plains, a place to stop only to take a break while traveling to the ski slopes of Colorado. But today's travelers will find that there are plenty of good reasons to visit the Panhandle city. Whether your interests are historic houses, shopping, or camping, you'll find a reason to make Amarillo a romantic destination.

Art lovers can't miss the **Amarillo Art Center** (2200 Van Buren St. on Amarillo College campus, 806-352-6513; free). This complex of three buildings (designed by the same architect who did the Kennedy Center in D.C.) features both visual and performing arts, with six permanent galleries devoted to changing and resident exhibits.

If you're a history buff, head to the nearby town of Canyon for a tour of the **Panhandle-Plains Historical Museum** (2401 4th Ave., 806-656-2244; admission fee). Texas's largest historic museum is filled with the things that have made Texas great, from the oil business to Western art.

But for shoppers, there's no place like Route 66. This stretch has 28 shops that feature collectibles. Eight antique malls boast nearly 120 dealers. Five bookstores stock hard-to-find titles. Thirty-one specialty shops feature jewelry, coins, vintage clothing, and records.

Start your visit at **Antiques Amarillo** (2700 W. 6th, 806-374-1066), an Art Deco–style building with a shiny silver front that harks back to the heyday of Route 66. Owners Ned and Donna Swygard have amassed a collection that ranges from antique furniture to delicate china to cowboy collectibles. Nearby, **Puckett Antiques and Collectibles** (2706 W. 6th, 806-372-3075) is the collection of Dorothy Puckett. This eclectic store has a little of everything—china, crystal, silver, furniture, dolls, and more. Across the street, the **6th Street Antiques Mall** (2715 W. 6th, 806-374-0459) has two stories of dealer goods, from Shawnee pottery to vintage hats to antique marbles. One of Amarillo's largest shops is the **Country Co-Op Mall** (2807 W. 6th, 806-372-4472), where over 60 dealers display their wares.

But these are all attractions you might expect to see in a tourist-friendly city like Amarillo. But there's one attraction that's truly unique: the **Cadillac Ranch** (west of town on I-40, no phone; free). This collection of 10 junkers representing the golden age of Route 66 is buried, nose down, at the same angle as Cheop's pyramid. This is a changing piece of artwork, assisted by travelers who have dotted the collection with graffiti. What might the Cadillac Ranch have to do with romantic traveling, you might ask? Well, the unusual attraction was a present from an oil man, Stanley Marsh 3, to his wife. (And you thought that you had received some strange gifts from your loved one!)

The Cadillac Ranch is unique to Texas, just like another attraction found outside the city limits. Amarillo is also the gateway to the nation's second largest canyon: Palo Duro. You can get a taste for the Old West with a visit to **Palo Duro Canyon State Park** (806-488-2227; admission fee). Truly a Texas-sized wonder, this natural canyon stretches 120 miles and drops 1,200 feet.

Couples can enjoy hikes along miles of trails or sit back and enjoy the view aboard the **Sad Monkey Railroad** (806-488-2222; admission fee), a miniature train that offers a two-mile narrated tour to the far reaches of the canyon.

Summer guests can enjoy **"TEXAS"** (806-655-2181, admission fee), an outdoor production that brings to life the struggles of the area's pioneers and native residents. The drama, produced against the backdrop of a 600-foot cliff, transports visitors back to the days of the Old West.

F Y I ✑

Getting There: Amarillo is located at the intersection of Interstates 40 and 27.

Festivals/Special Events: Texas Historic Route 66 Summer Festival is planned for the third weekend of June. Shop 'til you drop along 10 blocks of antique stores, bid at the antique auction, and have a taste of the chili cook-off. For more information, call (806) 374-0459.

Dining: In Amarillo, don't miss the Big Texan Steak House (I-40 Lakeside Dr. exit, 806-372-7000; $$–$$$, ☐). A tourist attraction as well as a fine steak house, this restaurant offers a free 72-ounce steak to anyone who can eat it in one hour. Along with good ol' Texas beef, they also serve exotic dishes such as rattlesnake and buffalo.

Love Nests: Amarillo is home to several B&Bs where couples can talk with fellow travelers, enjoy historic accommodations, and learn more about the Panhandle plains.

At Parkview Inn (1311 S. Jefferson, 806-373-9464; $, ☐) rooms vary from Colonial to country, but romantics should request the Victorian Rose Suite, with its own sitting area and reading niche with a fur rug.

The city's most elegant accommodation is the Galbraith House (1710 S. Polk, 800-NTS-POLK or 806-374-0237; $, □). Owned by Emmy award-winning opera singer Mary Jane Johnson and her husband David, this home is filled with memorabilia from its owner's stellar career. Posters of the singer's career with the Santa Fe Opera as well as autographed photos of Mary Jane with her costars fill the home. Her Emmy for *La Bohème* with Pavarotti and the Philadelphia Opera Company hangs in a second-floor sitting room.

The Galbraith House operates as a guest house without a resident manager. A full breakfast, which may include egg and sausage casserole, fresh granola, or homemade bread, is served by the innkeeper at a pre-arranged time. You'll have use of the country kitchen, as well as two sitting rooms, a living room with gas fireplace, and a lavishly paneled library filled with volumes displayed behind leaded glass doors. At the end of the day, snuggle beneath an antique quilt in one of the five rooms (each with a private bath).

The smallest B&B in town is Harrison House (1710 S. Harrison St., 806-374-1710; $, □). This classical Revival home has only one guest room, a sunny bedroom with antique furnishings and a large bathroom.

For More Information: Call the Amarillo Convention and Visitors Bureau at (800) 692-1338.

RUN FOR
THE BORDER

IF YOU'VE BEEN LONGING FOR A SOUTH-OF-
the-border getaway, then you're in luck—Texas offers
plenty of chances to enjoy a two-nation vacation.
Whether your goal is shopping, outdoor fun, dining,
nightlife, or just plain relaxation, the cities that straddle
the border serve up the romantic atmosphere that can
only be found in Mexico.

To brush up on what to expect when you cross the
border, see "Visiting Mexico" in the "Using This Guide"
section at the front of this book.

LAREDO–NUEVO LAREDO
Recommended for: shopping, nightlife, dining

The glassblower works with the molten glass, fresh from the 1,400-degree oven. In seconds, he blows air through a long rod, making the end of the molten glass look like a piece of fiery bubble gum. Quickly his assistant uses tongs to shape and roll it into a drinking glass, one that will be fired overnight and later sold to shoppers in Nuevo Laredo.

Hundreds of times of day, seven days a week, for over 20 years, this scene has been repeated at the **El Cid Glass Factory** (Avenida Reforma 3861), Nuevo Laredo's only glass factory and a magnet for shoppers looking for gifts that exhibit the quality of Mexican craftsmanship.

If you're looking for a weekend that combines some of Mexico's best shopping with a rich south-of-the-border atmosphere, then consider a trip to Nuevo Laredo and its sister city, Laredo. These cities are favorite destinations with Texas shoppers looking for quality, quantity, and bargains. But the bargains begin before you cross the international border. In Laredo, spend some time on Zaragoza Street, and enjoy a bazaar atmosphere where electronics, clothing, shoes, gold jewelry, and the world's finest perfumes are sold at a fraction of the retail price.

For Mexican imports such as pottery and wrought iron furniture, try the markets of the San Bernardo area a few blocks north of Zaragoza. The stores along San Bernardo are a good place to shop for larger import items if you won't be driving into Mexico. Shops like **Vegas' Imports** (4002 San Bernardo, 210-724-8251) are good stops.

But every shopper eventually heads for Nuevo Laredo and the seemingly endless procession of shops that line the avenues. From the moment you cross into Mexico, you'll be struck by the array of colors, merchandise, and sounds that define Old Mexico.

You'll reach the main avenue into Nuevo Laredo by crossing the Old Bridge or International Bridge No. 1. The bridge leads right onto Avenida Guerrero, the main shopping strip. Here you'll find merchandise whose price tags run the gamut from a dollar for trinkets from street vendors to thousands of dollars for fine jewelry at top-of-the-line shops.

Side by side, two of the city's top shops, **Marti's** (Avenida Guerrero) and **Deutsch & Deutsch** (Avenida Guerrero), tempt shoppers with the merchandise of fine department stores. Here you'll find the best that Mexico has to offer: handmade clothing, beautiful glassware, exquisite home furnishings, and spectacular paintings.

Just outside the doors of these elegant shops, you can buy a silver chain from a vendor for just a few dollars. Or head down the street to Nuevo Laredo's top shopping destination: the **New Market,** or **Nuevo Mercado.** The block long, open-air market is filled with shoppers every day. Its two floors contain over 100 small shops selling everything from jewelry to *serapes* to onyx chess sets. Be prepared to bargain at all the market shops. *Negociación* is a friendly game here, and both the merchant and the shopper usually go away happy.

Looking for silver jewelry? You'll see it of every description here—whether rope necklaces, dangle earrings, or cuff bracelets catch your eye. Look for sombrero earrings, bangle bracelets, and shrimp earrings, too. On all silver jewelry, check for the "925" stamp to ensure silver quality.

How about textiles? Colorful *serapes,* fringed blankets sporting bright stripes or native designs, and hand-embroidered Mexican dresses are other good buys. Leather goods including belts and wallets are always popular for the men in your family, sold at most of the market stores. Onyx chess sets, bookends, bowls, and fruit are also popular Mexican souvenirs.

FYI

Getting There: Laredo is 153 miles from San Antonio via I-35.

Festivals/Special Events: The biggest blowout of the year is, unusually enough, George Washington's birthday. Since 1898, both Laredo and Nuevo Laredo have partied on this day with elaborate floats and debutantes in exquisite gowns so large the young women travel to the evening balls not by carriage but by moving vans! The party spans 10 days of parades, balls, concerts, and fireworks every February.

In early July, Borderfest celebrates the seven flags that have flown over Laredo with live music, arts and crafts, food and parades.

Dining: So that you don't shop 'til you drop, take a break at one of Nuevo Laredo's restaurants or watering holes. Probably the best known establishment is El Dorado (Calle Belden and Avenida Ocampo, about two blocks from Nuevo Mercado; $, □), the former Cadillac Bar. A favorite watering hole since 1926 for many South Texans, it's the home of the Ramos Gin Fizz, a concoction of gin, lemon juice, and powdered sugar. The menu includes frog legs and red snapper.

One of the most elegant restaurants in town is Victoria 30-20 (Calle Victoria, near Nuevo Mercado; $–$$, □). Thick, aqua-tinted windows, a pastel interior, and a forest of plants adorn this remodeled home-turned-restaurant. Sip a beverage from a hand-blown glass and dine in air-conditioned comfort in one of Nuevo Laredo's most beautiful restaurants, specializing in Tex-Mex favorites such as *cabrito.*

For a taste of authentic Mexican food, try La Principal (Avenida Guerrero 624; $, □). Just a few blocks beyond the mercado, this restaurant is a favorite with Nuevo Laredo residents. It specializes in *cabrito,* with Mexican dishes such as *mollejas* (sweetbreads) and *sesos* (brains) served with *borracho* beans. Watch the chefs smoke the *cabrito* in the glassed-in kitchen, then enjoy the diner atmosphere with the locals.

In Laredo, the most romantic restaurant is the Tack Room (La Posada Hotel, 210-722-1701; $$–$$$, □) for fine dining in an elegant setting with a menu of seafood and steaks.

Love Nests: When we visit Laredo, we always head to our "home" at La Posada Hotel (1000 Zaragoza, 210-722-1701; $–$$, □). This hotel, literally located a stone's throw from the Rio Grande, just looks the way you expect a fine Mexican hotel to look, but with the ease and comfort of staying within the U.S. From its cool Saltillo-tiled lobby to its palm-shaded courtyards, this is one of the most romantic accommodations in Texas.

For More Information: Call the Laredo Convention and Visitors Bureau at (800) 361-3360. While in Laredo, drop by the offices at 501 San Augustin between 8 a.m. and 6 p.m. for brochures and refreshments.

DEL RIO–CIUDAD ACUÑA
Recommended for: fishing, houseboating, Indian cave paintings

When Frank Qualia came to Del Rio as a pioneer settler, the area reminded him of his homeland of Italy. Qualia reasoned that, if the two regions looked similar, perhaps this new home, like Italy, would also be a good site for a vineyard. He was right. Qualia created the **Val Verde Winery** (100 Qualia Dr., 210-775-9714; free), the first in Texas. Today it's still in operation and run by the fifth generation of the Qualia family. The rich soil and good growing conditions that attracted Qualia to Del Rio also draw vacationers.

Typically, when couples want bargains along the Texas-Mexico border, they head to Laredo. When they want semitropical warmth, they set their course for Brownsville. For mountains and big city activities, they drive to El Paso. But when travelers are looking for nature, history, movie excitement, camping, and fishing rolled into one, there's only one Texas border town that fills the bill: Del Rio. Perched on the Rio Grande almost directly west of San Antonio, this town of 35,000 calls itself "The Best of the Border," and works to fulfill that promise with attractions that draw visitors from around the country.

From the moment you see Del Rio, you'll realize that this city is different. More than any other border city, Del Rio is blessed with abundant water. Situated at the edge of the Chihuahuan Desert, the city is an oasis, lush with vegetation thanks to the **San Felipe Springs,** artesian wells gushing over 90 million gallons of water through the town daily. Spanish missionaries performed the first mass in Texas at these springs in 1635, christening the site *San Felipe del Río.* Later, settlers built a network of irrigation ditches to take advantage of the abundant water supply.

For a look at the founding residents of Del Rio, visit the **Whitehead Memorial Museum** (1308 S. Main St., 210-774-7568; free). This collection of early area buildings includes a replica of the Jersey Lilly, the infamous saloon where Judge Roy Bean dispensed his frontier justice. (The original Jersey Lilly is located northwest of Del Rio in Langtry.) Behind the saloon replica lie the graves of Judge Bean and his son, Sam.

Del Rio and Ciudad Acuña are separated by the Rio Grande, one of three rivers that form **Lake Amistad.** Amistad, derived from the

Spanish word for "friendship," was a joint project between Mexico and the U.S. The lake offers 1,000 miles of shoreline, tempting fishermen with bass, crappie, catfish, and striper. Separate fishing licenses are required for Mexican and American sides of the lake.

The best way to see the lake is aboard a boat, and the most luxurious ride is aboard a houseboat. With innumerable coves tucked inside sheer canyon walls, houseboaters can find seclusion as well as some beautiful, spring-fed swimming holes. Houseboats sleeping 4 to 12 people are rented by **Lake Amistad Resort and Marina,** a short drive from Del Rio.

Landlubbers will find plenty to see at the **Seminole Canyon State Park** (US 90, 9 miles west of Comstock, 915-292-4464; admission fee). Make your first stop the visitors center to learn more about the ancient culture that left this mysterious rock art.

Man first came to this area 12,000 years ago. These earliest residents stampeded bison over the canyon cliffs, the oldest known bison "jump" site of its kind in the country. Later climactic changes caused the bison to relocate. The weather grew hotter. Hunting was limited to deer and rabbits, and the Indians survived instead as foragers, living on sotol, prickly pear, and lechugilla.

The culture that made its home in this canyon 8,500 years ago produced the artwork now seen on guided tours. Sign up at the visitors center for the ranger-led walk to the **Fate Bell Shelter.** This rock overhang boasts the oldest rock art in North America, ochre, black, and white paintings whose exact meaning is unknown. One painting, known as "The Three Shamans," portrays three figures, one with antlers atop his head.

This park has some quiet campsites located high above the canyon. They offer a spectacular view of the Chihuahuan Desert, dotted with cactus and populated with numerous bird species.

East of Del Rio you'll also find many attractions. Fort Clark Springs was once the home of **Fort Clark,** built to protect the area from Indian attack. Today the stone barracks have been converted into modern motel rooms.

Fort Clark Springs is only a few miles from Brackettville, the home of the **Alamo Village** (FM 674 off US 90, 210-563-2580; admission fee). Remember John Wayne's version of *The Alamo*? It was filmed here in a replica of the Texas shrine that you can still tour today. Alamo Village is sometimes called the movie capital of Texas, and for good reason. Walk among its streets and you'll recognize buildings used in commercials, television shows, and many movies, as well as the popular mini-series *Lonesome Dove.*

Don't be surprised to see familiar faces here—the park remains open even when movies and so on are being shot. Take a tour of the buildings, some featuring movable walls to facilitate the work of film crews. You'll see a bank that has been the scene of numerous movie holdups, a working carriage shop, the John Wayne museum, and a church that even "explodes" on cue! And even if you miss the explosion, you'll have the chance to witness a "shootout" several times daily in front of the saloon.

Enjoy a root beer and a plate of Texas barbecue at the saloon, entertained by talented "showgirls" who perform Old West shows daily. These musical numbers are the result of talent searches conducted by Happy Shahan, the owner of Alamo Village. Shahan, a country musician himself, is seen at the park most days dressed in full cowboy regalia.

But every visit to the border must include a visit to neighboring Mexico, and in Del Rio that means a trip to **Ciudad Acuña.** To reach the international border and Ciudad Acuña, follow Garfield Avenue (Spur 239) west for three miles. Most travelers drive to the Texas side of the International Bridge and pay a small fee for secured parking. From there, you can take a cab across the river or walk across the toll bridge.

A bus carries shoppers from Del Rio across the border to Acuña's (pronounced "a-COON-ya") shopping district. This place is filled with tourist shops, especially along Hidalgo Street. There is no central market here, but the shops are continuous for several blocks as you enter town. For a round-trip trolley and bus schedule, call (210) 774-0580.

You'll find that shopping in Acuña is not as extensive as in Nuevo Laredo or Juárez, but nonetheless you'll find plenty of shops from which to choose. Shop for billfolds, *huaraches,* boots, saddles, gun holsters, and traditional Mexican purses, hand tooled with cactus, Aztec, and eagle designs at the leather shops, beautifully embroidered Mexican dresses, and knicknacks made of onyx.

F Y I ✍

Getting There: Del Rio is located about 150 miles west of San Antonio on US 90.

Dining: For an evening of dinner and dancing, visit Wright's Steak House (US 90, 3 miles west of the intersection of US 277, 210-775-2621;

$$, □). This casual steak house features all the usual cuts plus choices like Texas-sized chicken-fried steak. Save room for home-baked cheese-cake, then work off that big dinner on the dance floor. Live entertainment appears every Friday and Saturday night.

For an Old West atmosphere, check out the Cripple Creek Saloon (US 90 W., 210-775-0153; $$–$$$, □). Modeled after the original Cripple Creek Saloon in Colorado, this restaurant specializes in prime rib but also serves up a mean sirloin, filet mignon, and rib eye. Seafood, from lobster to Coho salmon to swordfish, rounds out the menu.

The most festive restaurant in the area is across the border at Crosbys (Hidalgo 195, 877-2-2020; $$, □). Both Americans and Mexicans frequent this lively restaurant for a good meal and a good time. From the etched glass and oak doors to the white columns separating the dining rooms, the look says "elegant" but the atmosphere definitely shouts "party." The menu features Tex-Mex food, steaks, seafood, and *de la presa la Amistad*—fish from nearby Lake Amistad. Try the *Camaron Relleno Estilo Crosbys* (shrimp stuffed with cheese and wrapped in bacon) or share a sampler platter, a massive tray of breaded quail, frog legs, stuffed shrimp, and beef strips. The margaritas are king-sized and served in glasses resembling goldfish bowls.

Love Nests: B&B lovers might check out the Foster House Bed and Breakfast (123 Hudson Dr., 210-775-9543; $, □). Located in an area once called "Lovers Lane," this is one of the oldest homes in the neighborhood lined with palm trees. Guests can select from four bedrooms, including the master suite with a queen-size bed, sitting room, screened porch, and private bath.

Bridal Bits: One of the most unique wedding sites in this part of the country is the Whitehead Memorial Museum (210-774-7568). Exchange vows beneath the archway in the courtyard or in the Spanish chapel dedicated to the area's early settlers. The museum can even arrange for catering and decorating.

For More Information: Call the Del Rio Chamber of Commerce at (800) 889-8149.

EL PASO–JUÁREZ
Recommended for: shopping, history, nightlife

Even before Marty Robbins sang about El Paso, this border city has held visitors' fascination. As the largest city on the U.S.-Mexico border, El Paso is a destination filled with south-of-the-border charm, big city excitement, and enough attractions to fill a quick day trip or a week-long vacation.

Texas's westernmost city is nestled in a ring of mountains, providing couples with one of the most romantic scenic drives in the state. Divided by the Franklin Mountains, El Paso is a city of almost two parts. View both parts as well as neighboring Juárez, Mexico, with a trip up Scenic Drive.

Scenic Drive (from Richmond St. on the east or Rim Rd. on the west side of the city; free) traces a winding course on the southern flank of Mount Franklin. Here, high above downtown, you get an unbeatable view from the scenic overlook. Another scenic route is the **Transmountain Road** or **Loop 375** (from I-10 northwest of city or US 54; free), which winds through Smugglers Gap and offers a good look at the surrounding countryside.

The cities seen from the Scenic Drive are members of different countries, but they are closely intertwined by both personal and business relationships. Many families straddle both sides of the border, and many American companies have *maquiladora* or twin plants for completing their products. A steady stream of truck traffic testifies to the importance of dual operations.

Another important industry in El Paso is the U.S. military. Home of **Fort Bliss,** established as an Army post nearly 150 years ago to protect against Indian attack, today many El Paso residents are employed by the military. For a look at the fort, visit some of the museums on the base, including the **Fort Bliss Museum** (Bldg. 5051, 915-568-4518; free), which depicts life here in the early days.

Several El Paso museums also display the cultural heritage and natural history of this area. The **El Paso Museum of History** (1-10 E and Ave. of the Americas N., 915-858-1928; free) recalls the history of El Paso through exhibits and dioramas. One of the city's premier exhibits is the **El Paso Museum of Art** (1211 Montana, 915-541-4040; free).

Here you'll find both Mexican and Southwestern art, plus the famous Kress collection of European artwork.

The history of this region included occupation by the Spanish, who developed a series of missions and *presidios* in the rugged area. The best way to view the missions is to hop aboard the **Trolley on a Mission** (1 Civic Plaza, 915-544-0062; admission fee), guided tours that offer a look at **Mission Ysleta** (the oldest mission in Texas), **Ysleta del Sur Pueblo** (a Tigua settlement, the oldest identifiable ethnic group in Texas), **Socorro Mission** (the oldest continuously active parish in the U.S.), and **San Elizario Presidio** (built on the famous Camino Real). The 4-1/2-hour tour includes lunch and shopping. You can also take in these missions on your own; pick up a free brochure from the **El Paso Convention and Visitors Bureau** as a guide to the sites.

No trip to El Paso would be complete without a journey to its sister city, **Juárez.** This historic community with over 1.2 million residents offers wonderful shopping opportunities just a few minutes away from El Paso. The largest Mexican city on the U.S.-Mexico border, Juárez is a vibrant metropolis. The easiest way to enter Mexico and to enjoy these neighboring shopping areas is aboard the **El Paso/Juárez Trolley Company** (915-544-0062; fee). The red-and-green trolleys depart from the El Paso Convention Center and many points throughout the city, then travel across the border to several sites in Ciudad Juárez.

You'll find both traditional *mercados* and modern malls here. The city's newest shopping area is the $20 million **Pueblito Mexicano** (Avenida Lincoln at Zempoala), a colorful blend of both a contemporary mall and a recreation of a Mexican *pueblito* or village. As you stroll along you'll find many of the same stores as at home, plus a few shops selling traditional *mercado* items such as woven blankets, onyx paperweights, and Mexican dresses.

For additional shopping, head down to Juárez's top two shopping districts: Avenida de las Americas and Juárez Avenue. Look for everything from leather goods to tequila to T-shirts.

A popular evening spot for tourists is the **Juárez Racetrack and Sportsbook** (Pan American Hwy., 915-775-0555). Watch greyhound races from the comfort of the air-conditioned clubhouse and enjoy drinks and dining at the modern facility.

FYI ✐

Getting There: El Paso is located on the westernmost end of Texas on I-10 and is served by the El Paso International Airport.

Nearby Attractions: "Nearby" in El Paso terms (which, in that respect, is closer to New Mexico's way of thinking) may mean 150 miles away. Distances here are generally measured not in miles but in hours. Many El Paso tourists take in sights throughout the region, including New Mexico's White Sands National Monument (98 miles north of El Paso off US 70, 505-479-6124; admission fee), the world's largest gypsum dune field with 300 miles of white sand. Another popular stop is the Guadalupe National Park (110 miles east of El Paso on US 62, 915-828-3251; admission fee) to enjoy the most rugged part of Texas through hiking and camping near Guadalupe Peak, the state's highest point. Carlsbad Caverns (145 miles northeast of El Paso on US 62) in New Mexico is a must for cave lovers. Texas skiers head to Cloudcroft, New Mexico (Hwy. 54, 505-682-2733 for ski information), as well as Ruidoso (Hwy. 54, 800-253-2255).

Festivals/Special Events: In January, enjoy the sounds of the El Paso Symphony Orchestra at the Chamber Music Festival (915-532-3776). Summer visitors can experience *VIVA El Paso!* (915-565-6900; admission fee), a musical staged in the open-air McKelligon Canyon Amphitheater. With a backdrop of the Franklin Mountains and a cast of over 50, the production covers the cultural evolution of El Paso, including the Indians, Spaniards, Mexicans, and cowboys.

Dining: El Paso's best known restaurant is actually located 30 minutes from the city (we told you that these folks didn't mind driving). Cattleman's Steakhouse at Indian Cliffs Ranch (30 minutes on I-10 E., take Fabens exit 49, and turn north for 5 minutes, 915-544-3200; $$$, ☐) serves up some of the state's best steaks in a huge complex that includes buffalo, a snake pit, and a children's zoo. Dress casually—this is a Texas-style steak house and it's got the steaks to prove it.

Another favorite of ours is Jaxon's Restaurant (1135 Airway at Viscount, 915-778-9696, or 4799 N. Mesa, 915-544-1188; $$–$$$, ☐). When El Paso residents are ready to celebrate a special event or to meet for a power lunch, they head to Jaxon's. This upscale restaurant recognizes both El Paso history and El Paso cuisine, a term that encompasses from chicken-fried steak to Tampico steak to fajitas and quesadillas. The walls of Jaxon's on Airway are filled with over 500 photos of the city and decorated with murals depicting the history of El Paso.

Love Nests: El Paso is home to many modern hotels including Camino Real Paso Del Norte (101 S. El Paso St., 915-534-3024 or 800-769-4300;

$$, □), with a wonderful lobby bar, and the Holiday Inn Park Place Hotel (325 N. Kansas St., 800-HOLIDAY; $, □). Both are located downtown and in easy walking distance to downtown shopping.

For More Information: Call the El Paso Civic, Convention, and Tourism Department at (800) 351-6024.

COASTAL GETAWAYS

WHEN WE THINK "VACATION," VISIONS OF THE coast often come to mind. The sun, surf, and sand make the Gulf coast a popular getaway, no matter what time of year. In spring and summer, this shoreline is filled with happy vacationers who come to play in the waves and enjoy an unbeatable beachside atmosphere. During fall and winter, the sun worshippers are replaced by a crowd that appreciates lower prices, temperate weather, and abundant bird life.

CORPUS CHRISTI AND PADRE ISLAND

Recommended for: beach fun, dining

The Coastal Bend has been a magnet for travelers since the days of buccaneers and Spanish *conquistadors.* Today, drawn by a relaxed atmosphere and a coastal beauty, visitors keep coming, turning this region into one of the state's top travel destinations.

For nearly every vacationer, the prime attraction is the Gulf shore. Over 113 miles of that shoreline stretch along Padre Island. Here, along the barrier island which over the years has sheltered the city of Corpus Christi from many hurricanes, you'll first reach a developed stretch of condos, shops, and restaurants, then miles of raw beach at the **Padre Island National Seashore.** Here couples can enjoy hours of seashell hunting without much competition on the solitary beaches. If you're lucky, you may find glass floats from distant fishing nets.

For all of Padre's beauty, many of the Coastal Bend's attractions of are of the man-made variety, especially in the city of Corpus Christi. The spot was charted in 1519 by Spanish explorer Alonzo Alvarez de Pineda, who named the bay "Body of Christ" (Corpus Christi). For several years, the coastal area was of interest mainly to pirates, men who used its bay and islands as hideouts.

Today Corpus Christi recalls its maritime history, and the discovery of the New World, at the **Corpus Christi Museum of Science.** You might never guess that Elvis Presley had a role in the creation of this world-class museum. (Concerned parents dreamed up the idea of the museum as a diversion away from Elvis during a concert visit to the city.)

Decades later, the museum is still attractive to families and visitors of all ages thanks to exhibits that include a natural history and science gallery, a shipwreck area where you can learn about a 1554 wreck and its victims, and a new exhibit area called Seeds of Change. Originally a Smithsonian display, this permanent exhibit now explains the impact of European discoverers on the New World.

"It really takes you through the environmental and cultural effects of the discovery," explains Lynne Dean. Along with the 10-minute video, visitors can see a recreation of a slave ship, take a peek in the Montserrat General Store, and learn about changes the discoverers brought, including corn, potatoes, sugar, horses, and disease. Those discoverers came to the New World by ship, so it's natural that the museum should be home to recreations of the Niña, Pinta, and Santa Maria. Docked beside the museum, the ships are open for boarding. The ships and the Seeds of Change exhibits provide a complete look at the time period. "There's nothing like this. It is truly the center of Spanish exploration and discovery," says Dean.

For maritime history of a more recent vintage, travel to the nearby **USS Lexington** (800-LADY-LEX; admission fee), the WWII aircraft carrier berthed just offshore. Allow at least two or three hours to fully appreciate the 16-story ship. You'll take a self-guided tour of the 42,000-ton behemoth, but volunteer guides (many who actually served on the *Lex*) are stationed throughout the ship. They'll be happy to give you personal insights into the ship which served from 1943 to 1991 and was nicknamed "The Blue Ghost." The Japanese Tokyo Rose claimed five times that the carrier had been sunk, but each time the rumor proved false. In the end, the carrier went on to serve longer than any other vessel in the U.S. Navy.

The *Lexington* is home to two bonus attractions: helicopter rides and a flight simulator. Both long and short helicopter rides off the flight deck provide a look at the city. Below, the first flight simulator in Texas gives visitors a chance to experience the sensation of a five-minute ride in a low flying jet.

After swooping through canyons and coastlines, take a walk from the *Lexington* to the **Texas State Aquarium** (2710 Shoreline Dr., 800-477-GULF; admission fee), where the focus is on sea life of the Gulf and the Caribbean Sea. Over 250 species of marine life are on exhibit here to give visitors a look at the creatures that live below the waves.

Couples also enjoy the **Art Museum of South Texa**s (1902 N. Shoreline Blvd., Bayfront Arts and Science Park, 512-884-3844; admission fee). Famous for its stark white architecture, this museum is filled with changing fine art exhibits of traditional and contemporary works. From the art museum, walk over to the **Watergardens** (Bayfront Arts and Science Park; free). Here a man-made stream tumbles from the entrance of the art museum down to a sunken circle of flags and fountains. This is a nice place to take a box lunch.

After a day of beaches and museums, test your luck at the **Corpus Christi Greyhound Race Track** (5302 Leopard St., 800-580-RACE;

admission fee). Take your chances here with a bet on these fast-as-lightning canines. The $21 million facility includes a food court and a clubhouse restaurant with an excellent view of the track from each table. (It's our favorite as the most romantic way to enjoy the races.) The basic entrance fee covers outdoor grandstand seating. During warmer months it's wise to spend a couple of extra bucks for air-conditioned reserved seating, which can be booked six days prior to the race.

F Y I

Getting There: Corpus Christi is the southernmost stop of I-37, located about 137 miles south of San Antonio.

Dining: Whenever we visit Corpus Christi, we make our first stop at the seafood restaurants. One of our favorites is Landry's Dockside (Peoples St. T-Head, 512-882-6666; $$, □). This restaurant is a restored two-story barge that sports a casual, fun atmosphere. Murals of fish span the walls, and huge picture windows offer a great view. The specialty of the house is Gulf seafood, including shrimp, oysters, and scallops. Another favorite is The Lighthouse Restaurant and Oyster Bar (Lawrence St. T-Head, 512-883-3982; $$, □). This popular restaurant is shaped like a small lighthouse. From inside, diners have a great view of sailboats on the bay and the Corpus Christi skyline. Seafood and steaks are the specialty here. And on shore, stop by the Water Street Oyster Bar (309 N. Water St., Water Street Market, 512-881-9448; $$–$$$, □). Located just a block from Shoreline Boulevard, this casual restaurant features Cajun-inspired seafood as well as the usual Gulf coast fare.

Love Nests: The most elegant hotel in the city is the Corpus Christi Marriott Bayfront (900 N. Shoreline Blvd., 800-874-4585; $$$, □). This elegant 474-room hotel overlooks the bay and includes a health club, swimming pool, and rooftop dining room. Many of Corpus Christi's main attractions lie within walking distance.

Bridal Bits: Corpus Christi is a goldmine of unique wedding sites. The most unusual is the Columbus Fleet (512-883-2862). Both the ships and the plaza are available for rental. If you want to be married out at sea, or at least out in the bay, *Captain's Clark Flagship* (512-884-1693) can be chartered for a wedding ceremony. Military buffs can rent the *USS Lex-*

ington (512-888-4873) for a truly Texas-sized wedding after hours. Art lovers can rent the Art Center of Corpus Christi (512-884-6406).

For More Information: Call the Corpus Christi Area Convention and Tourist Bureau at 800-678-OCEAN (6232).

GALVESTON
Recommended for: beachcombing, historic structures

Many cities offer fine dining, cultural events, and historical attractions. And beachside communities typically boast sun, sand, and surf. But Galveston is a marriage of the best of both worlds: city culture and seaside resort. This island paradise joins together fine dining, historical attractions, and cultural events normally found in the big city with the swimming and sunbathing of a beachside playground for a match made in heaven.

You'll find historical structures wherever you go on this island, and it's all the more surprising when you consider her stormy past. Galveston has weathered more than one hurricane, but the 1900 hurricane was by far the most devastating. Over 6,000 residents were killed by the storm, and many structures were demolished. This hurricane prompted city officials to begin work actually raising the island. That move plus the construction of a seawall today make Galveston a safe place to visit.

The historical district of the city is **The Strand,** an area that's today filled with vacationers enjoying specialty shops, outdoor dining, and around-the-clock excitement. In the late 19th century, however, this was the city's business district. Located a block away from the busy seaport, shippers unloaded merchandise from around the world and took a cargo of Texas cotton. Bankers and traders thrived on The Strand, which was often called the "Wall Street of the Southwest."

After the 1900 hurricane and the opening of the Houston Ship channel, Galveston lost its position as Texas's busiest seaport and The Strand was no longer a bustling center of commerce. Now, almost a hundred years later, The Strand holds the new title as one of the largest collections of historic buildings in the country. Things are hopping once again here.

Today The Strand is filled with restaurants, shops, and art galleries in an atmosphere that's right out of the 19th century. Gas street lights still illuminate walkways where couples can stroll hand-in-hand alongside restored ironfront buildings. To learn more about this National Historic Landmark District, you can enjoy a trolley ride or rent a walking tour cassette at the **Strand Visitors Center** (2016 Strand.)

The **Galveston Island Trolley System,** a $12 million operation, provides visitors with a romantic ride from the seawall to The Strand, with stops all along the way. It's an attraction that combines the best of the old and the new. The trolleys are strictly state-of-the-art, each one valued at nearly half a million dollars, but their look is purely turn of the century. Each trolley boasts interiors of cherry, mahogany, pine, and oak, and runs on fixed track, similar to the trolleys that ran along Galveston streets over 50 years before. (For a truly romantic view of this region, board a horse-drawn carriage at the corner of 21st and Strand.)

One of the most visited historic sites on the island is the **Moody Mansion and Museum** (2618 Broadway, 409-762-7668; admission fee). Completed in 1895, this was the home of the Moody family, one of the most prominent families in the Lone Star State. Building their fortunes in banking, ranching, and hotels, the family lived in lavish style. Today you can tour the stately manse and see the richly paneled rooms, stained-glass windows, and formal furnishings of its wealthy owners.

Just a few blocks away, Galveston's tall ship rests in port. The 1877 *Elissa* (Pier 21, 409-763-1877; admission fee) is open for self-guided tours. Stroll its decks and think back to a time when this ship was one of the most active in the world, sailing to some of the most remote areas of the British empire. Found in a Greek junkyard in 1974, the Galveston Historical Foundation steered a $4 million, 10-year renovation to return the vessel to its original condition.

After you tour the historic tall ship, have a look at the adjacent **Texas Seaport Museum** for the complete story of the *Elissa* and its rescue. The museum includes a database with the names of more than 130,000 immigrants who arrived in the U.S. at the port of Galveston. You can use computers here to see if any of your ancestors first stepped on American soil in "The Ellis Island of the West."

The prosperous shipping and banking industry in the late 1800s meant that the citizens had money to spend on recreation. Much of it was spent at the lavish **Grand 1894 Opera House** (2020 Post Office,

409-765-1894). Today, you can enjoy a tour of the Grand, or come by to see a classic film or to enjoy live entertainment.

History draws many visitors to Galveston, but one of its top attractions is also its newest. Spend a day at the **Moody Gardens** (Hope Blvd., 800-582-4673; admission fee) to watch a 3-D IMAX movie, pet exotic animals, romp on a white sand beach, or tour the 10-story glass Rainforest Pyramid. This one-acre conservatory brings the rain forests of Africa, Asia, and South America under one roof with plants, birds, and fish of the regions.

Of course, one of Galveston's top attractions is its beach. All of the coastline is comprised of public beaches. Look for parking along Seawall Boulevard. Several beach parks provide facilities, including **Steward Beach Park** (Seawall Blvd. at Broadway; admission fee). Lifeguards are on duty during the season.

If you're looking to get away, check out **Galveston Island State Park** (6 miles south of the city on FM 3005, 409-737-1222; admission fee). You'll find campsites as well as picnicking, fishing, and swimming in this park, which also offers good birding.

F Y I ✑

Getting There: Galveston is located about 45 minutes from Houston on I-45 and a two-mile causeway over the bay. From the east, you can arrive at the island via ferry from TX 87.

Festivals/Special Events: Typically, many people think of heading to island getaways during the spring and the summer. However, the winter months are some of Galveston's most active, thanks to her two big festivals, borrowed attractions that have thrilled millions of cold weather visitors.

In December, The Strand looks more like Old London during the weekends of Dickens on The Strand. Winter visitors stroll along the Strand in full Victorian dress during this festival.

Celebrate Mardi Gras in a 12-day festival with parades, beads, balls, and everything you'd expect to see in New Orleans.

Dining: Galveston's most elegant, and probably priciest, eatery is The Wendletrap (2301 Strand, 409-765-5545; $$$, ☐), where continental cuisine is served to a jacket-and-tie crowd.

Love Nests: You'll find all types of accommodations on Galveston Island. Some top choices are the Hotel Galvez (2024 Seawall, 800-392-4285; $$, □), the San Luis Resort and Conference Center (5222 Seawall, 800-445-0090; $–$$, □), and the Tremont House (2300 Ship's Mechanic Row, 800-874-2300; $–$$, □), located in the historic Strand district.

For More Information: Contact the Galveston Convention and Visitors Bureau at (800) 351-4236 in Texas or (800) 351-4237 outside the state.

SOUTH PADRE ISLAND
Recommended for: beach fun, border excursions

During the winter months, South Padre swells with vacationers from the northern states and Texas alike, all ready for a break from winter chills and post-holiday blues along some of the Lone Star State's most beautiful beaches. In the summer, South Padre is a place to play in lapping waves, enjoy a Tex-Mex atmosphere, and walk for miles on warm sand beaches.

Whether the calendar says winter or summer, the livin' is definitely easy on South Padre Island. Regardless of whether your escape here occurs in January or July, this is a destination that's ready-made for romance. You'll find candlelit restaurants serving the freshest seafood, wide avenues lined with majestic palms, and beaches where you can suntan, shell hunt, surf jump, or just saunter hand-in-hand.

Your visit to Texas's southernmost island begins with a drive over the **Queen Isabella Causeway,** the longest bridge in the state. It spans two and a half miles, starting at the base of the **Port Isabel Lighthouse.** Built in 1851, this beacon warned ships of landfall, casting a beam 16 miles into Gulf waters. During the Civil War, the tower was used by both Union and Confederate forces as a lookout post. Although the tower has been dark since 1905, visitors can tour the state historical park daily and climb the spiral staircase for the best view of the area.

And what a view it is. South Padre stretches for 34 miles, hugging the Texas coastline as a protective barrier against Gulf storms. At its widest point, the island is only a half mile across, providing every one of the 5,000 hotel rooms with an unbeatable view.

For some visitors, the chance to enjoy miles of pristine beach is reason enough to journey to South Padre. Miles of toasted sand invite travelers to enjoy horseback riding, sailboarding, surfing, sandcastle building, or just wave hopping in the surf. Don't miss a chance to go horseback riding with **Island Equestrian** (210-761-1809; admission fee), located just north of town. Beginner and advanced riders will enjoy a romp down the beach. And couples should look into the sunset rides, when you'll have a chance to ride up the dunes and watch the blazing orb vanish over Laguna Madre.

After the sun sets, the action continues across the island. With a spring break population that tops 120,000 annually, you can bet that South Padre Island has plenty of watering holes and festive nightlife. Some of the most popular watering holes are **Jake's Bar** (2500 Padre Blvd., 210-761-5012), **Louie's Backyard** (2305 Laguna Blvd., 210-761-6406), the **Padre Island Brewing Company** (Padre Blvd. and Bahama, 210-761-9585), **Boomerang Billy's** (2612 Gulf Blvd., 210-761-2420), **Wanna-Wanna** (5100 Gulf Blvd., 210-761-7677), **Wahoo Saloon** (210 W. Pike, 210-761-5344), and **Coconuts** (2301 Laguna Blvd., 210-761-4218). During the winter months, though, call ahead, as some establishments enjoy a vacation of their own during the quieter season.

Although everyone thinks of South Padre as a magnet for college students looking for a spring break party, few know that the island is a classroom for students at the **University of Texas Coastal Studies Laboratory** (210-761-2644; free). Research here focuses on coastal ecosystems, including a study of the sea turtles and dolphins that live in the area. You can stop by the lab Sunday through Friday for a look at aquariums filled with marine life.

For a further look at marine life (and even a chance to swim with some toothy denizens of the deep), stop by the island's newest attraction: the **South Padre Island Aquarium** (210-761-7067; admission fee), located across from Louie's Backyard. At the aquarium, peek through 42-inch portholes at sharks, rays, snapper, amberjack, and other Gulf species in the 104,000-gallon tank. But to really get eye-to-eye with these fishy friends, consider a swim in the shark cage. For 15 minutes, you can don a mask and snorkel and, within the safety of steel bars, swim in the warm water with the sharks and other marine life. The experience can also be videotaped. "We're the only place that actually puts people in the water with the sharks," says co-owner David Alvarez. "When people first get in, they're nervous, but after they're in a few minutes, they don't want to get out."

For another look at Gulf marine life, stop by the home of everyone's favorite South Padre resident, Ila Loetscher, at **Sea Turtle Inc.** (5805 Gulf Blvd.; small donation). Also known as the "Turtle Lady," Mrs. Loetscher has focused the attention of the world on Kemp's Ridley sea turtles through her conservation efforts. Today, volunteers run shows on Tuesday and Saturday at 10 a.m. to educate the public about these endangered turtles.

Regardless of your interests, you'll spend part of your visit along Padre Boulevard, the main street in town. This road is lined with restaurants, shell shops, and tourist facilities that can make your trip easier and more fun. Park your car and catch a ride on **"The Wave,"** a motorized trolley that stops at attractions along the way. Tickets are just 50 cents a ride or a dollar for the entire day.

Just 25 minutes from the international border, South Padre calls itself the "Two Nation Vacation." Save time for a day trip to Brownsville and Matamoros. The southernmost city in Texas, Brownsville features one of the top 10 zoos in the country. The **Gladys Porter Zoo** (Ringgold and 6th Sts. in Brownsville, 210-546-2177; admission fee) is home to 1,900 animals, most contained by waterways rather than fences.

From Brownsville, it's a quick five-minute walk across the International Bridge to **Matamoros, Mexico.** Follow TX 48 downtown to the convention center and park at the free municipal lot. After crossing the bridge, it's a short taxi ride to the *mercado.* Here you can bargain for silver jewelry, leather goods, glassware, blankets, *serapes,* Baja jackets, and onyx creations.

F Y I ✍

Getting There: To reach South Padre Island, travel I-37 south toward Corpus Christi. Just 15 miles before reaching Corpus Christi, turn south on US 77 and continue south. Air service to the Valley is through Harlingen's Valley International Airport and Brownsville's South Padre International Airport.

Dining: You'll find a good selection of restaurants on South Padre Island. For seafood, the most elegant and romantic stop is Scampi's Restaurant (206 W. Aires, 210-761-1755; $$–$$$, □). Dine on fresh seafood (don't miss the award-winning peanut butter shrimp—a spicy dish), steaks, and pasta as you view the sunset over Laguna Madre. After dinner, dance to live music in the club upstairs.

A more casual spot for seafood is Amberjack's Bayside Bar and Grill (209 W. Amberjack, 210-761-6500; $$, □). The festive restaurant also has a good sunset view from both the downstairs eatery and the upstairs bar.

Other popular restaurants include Blackbeards' (103 E. Saturn at Padre Blvd., 210-761-2962; $$, □) for steak, seafood, and burgers; Jesse's Cantina and Restaurant (2700 Padre Blvd., 210-761-4500; $$, □) for Tex-Mex; and Louie's Backyard (2305 Laguna Blvd., 210-761-6406; $$, □) for seafood and prime rib followed by after-dinner dancing with a sunset view.

An excellent lunch spot is the Padre Island Brewing Company (Padre Blvd. and Bahama, 210-761-9585; $$, □) for burgers, shrimp tacos, and beer brewed on-site.

Our favorite breakfast spot is Rovan's Bakery Restaurant and BBQ (5300 Padre Blvd., 210-761-6972; $, □). Good enough to warrant a trip to South Padre, this restaurant features home-style breakfasts, from platters to pecan waffles to biscuits and gravy. Now expanded, the original section features miniature trains that run on tracks above diners' heads.

Love Nests: Regardless of your budget, you'll find an accommodation on South Padre Island. Most properties are condominium complexes: the island offers over 45 condominium hotels on the Gulf side, over 20 on the inner island, and nearly a dozen properties on the bayside. This compares to 10 Gulf-side hotels and motels, 6 inner island properties, and 3 hotels and motels on the bayside.

Top-of-the-line properties include the Sheraton Beach Resort (210 Padre Blvd., 800-222-4010 or 210-761-6551; $$$, □), Radisson Resort (500 Padre Blvd., 210-761-6511; $$$, □), and Bridgeport Condominiums (334 Padre Blvd., 800-221-1402; $$$, □).

If you're on a budget, check out the Motel 6 (4013 Padre Blvd., 210-761-7911; $, □), Days Inn South Padre Island (3913 Padre Blvd., 210-761-7831; $, □), and Best Western Fiesta Isles (5701 Padre Blvd., 800-528-1234; $, □).

For More Information: Call the South Padre Convention and Visitors Bureau at (800) 343-2368, or stop by the Visitors Center at 600 Padre Boulevard.

PORT ARANSAS
Recommended for: beach walks, seafood restaurants, beachfront condos

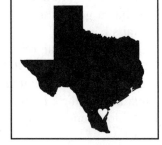

Some coastal towns exist for the fishing industry. Others support the shipping world. But Port Aransas is best known as just a place to have fun. Life in the coastal community centers around the Gulf, with its crying gulls, rolling surf, and miles of pancake-colored sand.

"The beach itself is our main attraction," explains Carol Ann Anderson, president of the Port Aransas Tourist and Convention Bureau. "We have open beaches allowing people to camp, cook out, or drive on the beach. Also, our shelling is more than a little better than other coastal cities."

Although Port A is now one of the state's most popular coastal destinations, its history as a hideaway dates back far before the days of sunscreen and surfboards. Some of the island's first residents were the fierce Karankawa Indians, a cannibalistic tribe that greeted later visitors, from pirates to Spanish missionaries. Buccaneer Jean Lafitte reputedly camped on the shores of **Mustang Island,** building bonfires to lure ships seeking a pass onto the beach to be looted and plundered. Wild horses, evolved from the steeds of Spanish explorers, gave Mustang Island its name.

Just as it was over 200 years ago, the most common way to reach Port A is by water. Follow TX 361 from Aransas Pass across the Redfish Bay causeway to **Harbor Island.** A ferry runs 24 hours daily from Harbor Island across the **Corpus Christi Ship Channel** to Port Aransas. On weekends during peak season and holidays, there can be a long wait for the ferry. Tune your radio to 530 AM for ferry traffic conditions during the morning, lunch hour and late afternoon rush times.

Few coastal cities offer more **fishing cruises** than Port Aransas. In varying seasons, the Gulf is home to mackerel, ling, pompano, marlin, barracuda, grouper, and amberjack. In the calmer bay waters, look for redfish, speckled trout, drum, and flounder.

Large group trips, taking as many as 100 passengers, provide bait and tackle, and cost about $20 a day. A fishing license is not required for the deep sea excursions since you will be fishing in out-of-state waters. These big cruises are great for families and budget travelers. Serious fishermen looking for big game fish such as marlin and shark should book charter excursions for personalized service.

Remember, love takes a back seat to seasickness. If you do take a fishing cruise, be aware that Gulf waters can be very choppy. Except for the bay cruises, most boats travel 15 to 20 miles from shore. Seas are usually calmest in the summer but even then four- to six-foot waves are possible. Seasickness has spoiled more than one couple's cruise, so be sure to purchase motion sickness medication from your doctor before your trip.

If your idea of a good catch would be a glimpse of feathers rather than fins, Port Aransas also has a bird watching cruise. The **M/V Wharf Cat** (512-749-5760 or 800-782-BIRD; admission fee), a 75-foot heated and air-conditioned catamaran, departs from **Fisherman's Wharf** every Monday and Tuesday during the winter through late March for a look at the magnificent whooping cranes. (On other days, the cruise departs from nearby Rockport.) The cruise leaves Port Aransas for the **Aransas National Wildlife Refuge,** the winter home of the five-foot-tall whooping cranes. Binoculars and scopes are provided, along with checklists of frequently spotted birds.

To learn more about the plant and animal life that make this area home, leave time for a weekday visit at the **University of Texas Marine Science Institute** (1 Ship Channel, 512-749-6720; free). Students of oceanography, ecology, marine chemistry, and botany are trained at this branch of the University of Texas. Located on 82 beach-front acres, the Visitors Center is open to the public, and features exhibits and films on Texas Gulf life.

Of course, the best way to learn about the beach life is to become part of it. And that's just what most visitors do. Armed with sunscreen, beach umbrellas, and folding chairs, they line the Gulf beach where swimmers and surfers frequent the shallow, warm waters and beachcombers search for fragile sand dollars, pieces of coral, and unbroken shells. Drivers on the public beach are restricted to a marked lane, and parking requires an annual permit, available from the Chamber of Commerce or at many Port Aransas businesses. There is free boardwalk access to the beach from many of the condominiums as well.

Although cars are permitted on the **Port Aransas beach,** vehicles are restricted to parking areas at **Mustang Island State Park** (Park Rd. 53, southwest of Port Aransas, 512-749-5246; admission fee), so the beach here is a little quieter. The facilities at this scenic beach include freshwater showers, picnic tables, and tent and RV camping.

Both Port Aransas and Mustang Island State Park beaches are popular with vacationers, but if you're looking for a real getaway, head to nearby **St. Jo Island.** You'll feel like pirate Jean Lafitte, whose camp was found on the island in 1834. Large iron rings, thought to have been used to tie up small boats his group used to row ashore, were discovered at the site. Even today, the island is accessible only by boat, and there are no public facilities.

St. Jo is a quiet getaway for fishing, beachcombing, swimming, or shelling. Ferries leave throughout the day from **Woody's Boat Basin** (512-749-5252; admission fee), so you can stay as long as you like.

F Y I 〰

Getting There: Port Aransas is located northwest of Corpus Christi. Ferries at Harbor Island in Aransas Pass provide transportation into Port Aransas.

Festivals/Special Events: There's no bigger annual event on the Texas coast than spring break, and 150,000 students head to Port A for this annual rite. If you're looking for a quiet (or anything resembling quiet) getaway, skip this time of the year. Call the Convention and Visitors Bureau to find out the peak arrival time for hyperactive spring-breakers.

Dining: Pull up a dockside seat at Tortuga Flats (Trout St., near Fisherman's Wharf, 512-749-5255; $$, □) and enjoy an oyster "po'boy," shrimp basket, or burger. Dig into a steaming bowl of shrimp, sausage, potatoes, stone crab claws, and crawfish at the Crazy Cajun (315 Alister St., 512-749-5069; $$, □), or enter a geodesic dome and dine on spaghetti primavera, shrimp and pepper pasta, or Cajun-style blackened redfish at the Seafood and Spaghetti Works (710 Alister St., 512-749-5666; $$, □).

Love Nests: You won't find towering, full-service hotels in Port A, but just about every other type of accommodation is available. Many condominiums include full kitchens and appliances, and boardwalk access to the beach. High rises like Sandcastle Condominiums (Sand Castle Dr., 800-727-6201; $$, □) and, located out of town, the Mayan Princess Condominiums (Hwy. 361, 800-662-8907; $, □) offer oceanfront rooms with a view and easy access to the beach.

The most historic hotel on the island, and a part of the National Register for Historic Places, is the Tarpon Inn (200 E. Cotter St., 800-365-6784; $, □), dating back to 1923. The lobby walls are papered with thousands of tarpon scales, each autographed by the lucky fisherman. There's even a scale signed by Franklin Roosevelt. Within the last two years, the hotel has been completely renovated, but still preserves the breezy atmosphere with rockers on the verandas. Each of the 23 rooms is uniquely decorated and furnished with antiques.

For More Information: Call the Port Aransas Tourist and Convention Bureau (800) 45-COAST.

FESTIVALS
FOR LOVERS

READY, SET, PARTY! IF THERE'S ONE STATE that knows how to throw a fiesta, it's the Lone Star State. From the coastal plains to the East Texas forests to the West Texas mountains, Texas is a party in progress.

For a free quarterly guide to Texas festivals, write the Texas Department of Transportation at P.O. Box 5064, Austin, TX 78763-5064, or call (800) 8888-TEX.

RENAISSANCE FESTIVALS

"My lords and ladies, get ye to the Texas Renaissance Festival!" Beginning at the end of September, this Texas-sized celebration transports visitors back to the days of King Henry VIII. Here you can step into a fantasy world where the king and 500 subjects pass through the streets at noon, where jesters and jugglers provide a colorful entertainment at every turn, where craftsmen rekindle  ancient skills, and where Anne Boleyn once again loses her head for you-know-who.

Located near Houston between Plantersville and Magnolia, the **Texas Renaissance Festival** is the largest such festival in the country. Over its seven-weekend run, the event draws 250,000 visitors and grosses $2.4 million. The fairgrounds are transformed into a medieval world with 300 permanent structures all constructed in the true Tudor style.

Budget an entire day to take in this spectacle (and a whole weekend if you intend to enjoy several shows). Just covering the entire pine-shaded grounds takes time, and, in true Renaissance style, you don't want to rush à la 1990s. And don't be shy about arriving bedecked in medieval regalia. Many guests blend right in, so much so that craftsmen and actors are identified with leather badges.

One way to step back to this long-ago time is by attending the **Feast of Earthly Delights,** a two-hour event that combines a six-course meal with rollicking and sometimes bawdy entertainment. Between courses, guests (each sporting a red or blue hat, some with multiple points) enjoy entertainment by Merlin the Magician, belly-dancers, a tightrope walker, and musicians. Those who don't partake in the feast will find plenty of good food throughout the park, from turkey legs to shrimp kabobs, washed down with red wine or a mug of ale.

Authentic arts and crafts fill the booths throughout the festival. Look for glassblowers, jewelry makers, leather workers, candlemakers, potters, and more. Over 250 permanent shops are positioned throughout the grounds.

Equally authentic are the **shows,** scheduled throughout the day at stages across the park. Mud wrestlers. Jousters. Chariot races. Magic shows. Over 40 games and rides also tempt visitors. Here's your chance for the two of you to be lost in the Mystery Maze or to enjoy a ride together on an elephant or camel.

F Y I ✐

Getting There: Festival grounds are located between Plantersville and Magnolia on FM 1774, northwest of Houston. From Houston, take I-45 north, turn left on 105, turn left on FM 1774 at Plantersville, and then drive six miles to the grounds. Parking is free.

Bridal Bits: If you've ever had visions of a wedding Romeo and Juliet–style, here's a wonderful opportunity. Fantasy wedding packages are available for any weekend. While at the festival, we witnessed a beautiful ceremony held in the center of the festival grounds. Following a procession of costumed actors representing friars, Anne Boleyn, and ladies-in-waiting, the bride arrived in a horse-drawn coach. Her arrival at the ivy-covered wedding bower was heralded by the sound of trumpets. Guests sat on simple benches, and following the exchange of vows (performed by a costumed minister), the party enjoyed a feast of medieval foods.

For More Information: Call (800) 458-3435 for general information and ticket prices. Reservations are required for the Feast.

Other Medieval Festivals:

Arlington: On the first weekend of December, enjoy the Feast of Carols Renaissance Festival at the University of Texas at Arlington. Revelers can dine on traditional dishes like pork medallions with apple chutney, butternut squash, and plum pudding while enjoying trumpet fanfares, costumed performers, and holiday carols. Admission fee; (817) 273-2962.

Waxahachie: Enjoy juggling and jousting, shop for crafts made by 200 artists, and dine on turkey legs and peasant bread at Scarborough Faire, an annual festival held south of Dallas. Late April to mid-June, weekends only. Admission fee; (214) 938-1888.

WINE FESTIVALS

Wine lovers, take note: The oldest and largest wine festival in Texas is held, appropriately enough, in the town of Grapevine. Best known as the home of the Dallas/Fort Worth International Airport, Grapevine is a popular destination for antique shoppers and history buffs, but it's also top of the list for wine connoisseurs. During the second weekend in September, the city celebrates the

wines of Texas with **Grapefest,** a three-day event that draws 85,000 people.

The most popular event at the festival is the **People's Choice Wine Tasting.** Over 2,500 people generally participate in the event, which allows the public to judge their favorite wines. Other popular events include the **Vintners' Auction Classic,** educational wine seminars, and a celebrity wine judging.

The most elegant event is the **Texas Wine Tribute,** a black-tie gala that features Texas wines and gourmet dining. Over 150 tuxedoed sommeliers and servers staff the function, which features 10 premium wines.

Grapevine holds true to its moniker as it's home to four wineries and tasting rooms. **Delaney Vineyard and Winery, La Buena Vida Vineyards, La Bodega Winery,** and **Homestead Winery** call the region home. (Frequent flyers will appreciate La Bodega, known as the first tasting room ever to operate in a major U.S. airport. When you have time to kill in Terminal 2E near Gate 6, check out the tasting room.)

F Y I 🍃

Getting There: Grapefest is held in Grapevine's Main Street Historic District just off Highway 114, two exits west of the North Entrance to the Dallas/Fort Worth International Airport.

For More Information: Call the Grapevine Convention and Visitors Bureau at (800) 457-6338.

Other Wine Festivals:

Austin: In April, the Texas Hill Country Wine and Food Festival brings in culinary and wine experts for several days of tastings and seminars. (512) 329-0770.

Dallas: In early September, the Best of Texas Festival invites visitors to sample Texas food and wines and shop for Texas-made products. (214) 824-4226.

Fredericksburg: Enjoy local wines and foods at the Fredericksburg Food and Wine Festival, held in late October on Market Square. (210) 997-8515.

Grapevine: In late April, celebrate the flowering of the vine and the official release of Texas's new vintages at the New Vintage Wine and Food Festival. Events include a four-course brunch, a gourmet food show and seminar, a black-tie Texas Gourmet Gala Dinner, seminars on food and wine, and a two-hour tasting featuring Texas wines and local foods. (800) 457-6338.

San Angelo: In early April, sample Texas wines and foods at the Texas Wine Festival. (915) 653-6793.

HARVEST FESTIVALS

Since the days of Adam and Eve, apples have held a special attraction for lovers. In Texas, there's no better place to tempt your partner with varieties that range from Red Delicious to exotic Jonagold than the community of Medina.

Today Medina is recognized as the capital of the Texas apple industry, a business that took root in 1981 when Baxter Adams and wife Carol moved to Love Creek Ranch outside of Medina. It's a land of rocky, rugged hills, with fertile valleys irrigated by the cool waters of Love Creek, a spring-fed creek that originates on the ranch.

These valleys gave Adams the idea for an orchard, an orchard which would not take a great deal of land. He hit upon an idea: smaller is better. This Texas version of Johnny Appleseed specializes in dwarf apple trees, plants which reach a height of only five or six feet. The Lilliputians boast full-size apples, however, up to 50 pounds per tree, in varieties from the common Red Delicious to the unusual Gala and Crispin.

Baxter and Carol started with just 1,000 trees in 1981, and they were soon in the apple business. Unlike the full-sized trees that take seven years to produce a crop, the dwarfs yield fruit in just a year and a half. Another advantage Adams has over the northern producers is his growing season. Texas apples ripen weeks before their Northern cousins.

It's easy to see that this just isn't a business for Baxter Adams, it's a challenge. When he walks down a row of Red Delicious, he stops to polish one of the crimson fruits. "I just love that color. So many people told us 'You can't grow apples in Texas because they won't turn red.'" Adams laughs and pulls the bright red apple from the tree, taking a crunchy bite.

Growers who come to the area soon find that it's a town operation, with nearly all of Medina taking part. This is a one-street town, but there's no mistaking its apple connection. The Adams Apple Company is downtown Medina. The processing plant stays busy from July through October, and the Cider Mill Store is filled year around. The store offers apple jelly, apple jam, apple syrup, and apple shampoo. Not to mention a terrific apple ice cream.

Every July, the Hill Country celebrates this blooming industry with the **International Apple Festival.** What began as an orchard party has become a festival with 20,000 participants. The party begins the night before with a street dance and continues the next day with activities for the whole family. Activities include contests for the best apple, best apple pie, and best apple anything. There is also a quilt contest, volleyball championship, and, for the really energetic, a "triapple-on." Arts and crafts booths tempt shoppers with homemade items. Continuous entertainment keeps up the festive mood with performers on three stages.

"I feel like Medina's a special place," says Baxter Adams, looking out on the Medina storefronts—the Cider Mill, the Adams Apple headquarters, the processing plant, and the apple festival offices. "I think Love Creek's had a good impact on Medina, and the people of Medina have been very supportive of Love Creek and the apple business. It's been a very happy marriage."

FYI

Getting There: Medina is located northwest of San Antonio on TX 16.

For More Information: For information on tours of Love Creek Ranch or on the International Apple Festival, call (210) 589-2588.

Other Harvest Festivals:

Luling: Enjoy the fruit of the summer at the Watermelon Thump. With a beer garden, evening street dances, arts and crafts, a barbecue cookoff, and more. Late June. (210) 875-3214.

Mission: Travel to the Rio Grande Valley for a taste of Texas's sweet Ruby Red grapefruit at the Texas Citrus Fiesta Celebration. Late January to early February. (210) 585-2727 or 585-9724.

Poteet: What do you get when you mix one of Texas's sweetest products with some of the biggest names in country music? A berry good time, that's what. The Poteet Strawberry Festival preserves a 48-year tradition celebrating the annual harvest of the South Texas strawberry crop with music, dances, and plenty of homegrown fun. The massive scale of the berry bash is impressive on its own, but it's astounding considering the size of Poteet. This town located 30 minutes south of San Antonio on Texas 16 has a population of only 3,000. Many town residents volunteer their time to help make the festival a success. They are joined by volunteers from around the state, and often from around the country and even from foreign nations. Over 8,000 volunteers work to coordinate this Texas-sized festival. Early April. (210) 276-3323 or 742-8144.

Stonewall: It's called the "Peach Capital of Texas," and every June Stonewall is ripe with fun and festivities. Located between Johnson City and Fredericksburg on US 290, Stonewall is happy to share its fuzzy treasure at this yearly celebration. Activities include a rodeo, arts and crafts, food booths, and dances. Third weekend of June. (210) 644-2735.

MUSIC FESTIVALS

For Texans, there's one sure sign of approaching summer: the Kerrville festivals. Just as dependable as spring bluebonnets, fall leaves, or winter's chill, these seasonal signposts herald summer with song, art, and just plain fun. For over two and a half decades, Kerrville has been home to the Kerrville Folk Festival and, at the same time, the Texas Arts and Crafts Fair. Located northwest of San Antonio on I-10, Kerrville swells with crowds from around the Southwest during this season as folks come in for a celebration of art in many forms.

Music lovers will find plenty of fun in late May and early June at the **Kerrville Folk Festival,** an 18-day spectacle of song held nine miles south of Kerrville at the Quiet Valley Ranch. That valley is anything but quiet, however, during these sell-out concerts that feature the finest in folk performers.

Bring a lawn chair along with some comfortable clothes for this event (and a rain hat in case the clouds are looming, because, rain or shine, the concerts go on). Bottles, cans, glass containers, ice chests, and pets are not permitted on the festival grounds. If you don't want to miss a beat, free camping is available to anyone buying tickets for three or more days (or a single night of camping can be purchased for $4 per person). A 20-acre campground with picnic tables, restrooms, solar-heated showers, and a country store help many visitors turn the event into a vacation filled with memories of afternoons and evenings of folk performances and late night campfires. Food and beverages may be brought into the campgrounds.

While you're in Kerrville, don't miss the **Texas State Arts and Crafts Fair,** an extravaganza featuring over 200 top Texas artists and craftspersons. For these two weekends, the grounds of Kerrville's Shreiner College are filled with jewelry, sculpture, paintings, textiles, leatherwork, pottery, and more. Spread across 16 acres, the festival gives visitors a chance not only to shop but to meet with the artists themselves. Selection of the artists is done carefully so that the fair features only the best in Texas artwork. No manufactured, mass produced, or molded items are permitted, and all the artists must reside in Texas.

F Y I ✑

For More Information: For more information on the Folk Festival, call (210) 257-3600. The ticket hotline is (800) 435-8429. To learn more about the Arts and Crafts Fair, call the Texas Arts and Crafts Educational Foundation at (210) 896-5711. For brochures on other Kerrville attractions or accommodations, call the Kerrville Convention and Visitors Bureau, (800) 221-7958.

Other Music Festivals:

Athens: Kick up your heels at the Texas Fiddlers' Contest and Reunion, a celebration that dates back to the 1930s. Always the last Friday in May. (903) 675-2325 or 675-1859.

Austin: Clubs throughout the city feature groups from around the country during South by Southwest Music and Media Conference. Mid-March. (512) 467-7979.

Top name entertainers perform on the banks of Town Lake during Aquafest, the capital city's summer send-off. Early August. (512) 472-5664.

Port Arthur: Celebrate the '60s at the Janis Joplin Birthday Bash. Mid-January. (800) 235-7822.

WILDFLOWER FESTIVALS

In some parts of the country, April showers bring May flowers. In the Hill Country, those showers come with April bluebonnets—the only sure sign of spring a real Texan will accept. During early April, the Hill Country celebrates those spectacular blooms with the **Highland Lakes Bluebonnet Trail.** This self-guided tour winds through small lake-side communities and roadside displays of  the flowers. What began over 30 years ago simply as a drive from one bluebonnet field to another has blossomed into one of Central Texas's major events, drawing bus tours, photographers, and vacationers. Don't be surprised to see 30 or 40 cars pulled off the road at some spots, with children kneeling in neck-high fields of lupinus, better known as blue-bonnets, smiling for the family camera.

The Bluebonnet Trail begins in the capital city of **Austin.** Highways leading in all directions are lined with miles of bluebonnets and other wildflowers thanks to the efforts of the Texas Highway Department and Lady Bird Johnson, whose highway beautification program is partially responsible for the profusion of wildflowers.

Austin is home to the **National Wildflower Research Center** (4801 LaCrosse Ave., 512-292-4200), a research facility whose goals are to educate the public about the importance of wildflowers. The Center boasts greenhouses, test plots, and an auditorium where audiovisual presentations are featured. Have a question about wildflowers? Feel free to ask the botanists on staff. During the first Bluebonnet Trail weekend, volunteers will operate a booth to answer questions about Texas's most colorful natural resource.

From Austin, follow the Bluebonnet Trail by taking US 183 north to FM 1431 West, a scenic drive that is your gateway to the rolling, rocky Hill Country. The first stop on the trail is the small town of **Marble Falls,** perched on the bluffs of the Colorado River. Marble Falls hosts an excellent art show sponsored by the Highland Arts Guild. At this show and others on the trail, you'll find many bluebonnet paintings—in every size and description. You can take home a souvenir bluebonnet painting on anything from a coffee cup to a sawblade, all done by Central Texas artists. In all, the Highland Lakes area boasts over 500 artists whose crafts include oil painting, stained glass, jewelry, photography, and granite painting. Year around, the **Highland Arts Guild** displays and sells its wares at a gallery located at 318 Main Street, downtown.

Head on down FM 1431 to the hamlet of **Kingsland.** Perched on the banks of Lake LBJ, Kingsland was the site of the last Indian battle in this region. An area rich in Indian lore, one beautiful tale describes the origin of the bluebonnet. The story goes that one summer the land was dry, and the buffalo had no food to eat. Soon, the Indians were faced with starvation.

The Great Spirit spoke to the chief in a vision, and said that the rains would come if the tribe sacrificed its most precious possession to the Great Spirit. Fine horses and beautiful bonnets were offered, but no rains came. One evening, a small girl sacrificed her favorite corn husk doll, tearfully laying it upon the coals of the sacrificial fire. With morning came life-giving rain and a miracle—the dry fields were covered with grass for the starving buffalo. And everywhere that the ashes of the fire had blown grew a carpet of beautiful blue flowers: the bluebonnet.

To celebrate those blooms, Kingsland hosts several special events, including an arts and crafts show hosted by the Highland Arts Guild on both weekends at the **Kingsland House of Arts and Crafts.** Many of the bluebonnet festivities are centered near **Lake Buchanan,** the first and largest lake in the Highland chain. Contained by one of the largest multiple-arch dams in the world, this lake spans 23,000 acres. Walk out on the dam for a look at sunning turtles along its edges, but save time to tour a free museum located here. It traces the development of the Highland Lakes chain and includes exhibits on native animals and fish.

The Chamber of Commerce office is located next door to provide you with maps and brochures.

The village of **Buchanan Dam** is home to the oldest artists' cooperative in the country and sponsors a large art show during the festival. Wander among the booths and shop for inexpensive bluebonnet paintings and crafts for sale under the shade of large oak trees next to the gallery. Step into the gallery for a look at fine bluebonnet paintings. The cooperative is located on TX 29 one mile west of Buchanan Dam.

The largest town near Lake Buchanan is **Burnet,** and it's the host of several Bluebonnet Trail events. Burnet celebrates with everything from bed races to arts and crafts, as well as marathons for the energetic. For children, there's kite decorating, face painting, pet shows, and Hot Wheels races.

From Burnet, head to the westernmost point of the Bluebonnet Trail: **Llano.** The site of Indian raids a century ago, this small town hosts tours of historic homes, an art show, and a festival during Bluebonnet Trail weekends. Llano artists exhibit their works in the **Llano Fine Arts Guild Gallery** at 503 Bessemer (TX 16). Take a Chamber of Commerce walking tour of the historic district, then stop by the American Legion Hall to stomp your feet to the sounds of the annual Old Time Fiddle Fest. From Llano, you can return to San Antonio by continuing south on TX 16 to the intersection of I-10.

F Y I ≫

Nearby Attractions: The best way to view the wildflowers without the traffic is aboard the *Hill Country Flyer* (512-477-8468; admission fee), a 1916 restored passenger train. Step aboard the refurbished passenger cars, hold onto your hat, and get ready to roll through the Hill Country.

Every weekend, the *Hill Country Flyer* transports visitors on a round-trip excursion through the oak- and cedar-dotted hills to the town of Burnet. Cedar Park, a small town on US 183 northwest of Austin, is the starting point for the 33-mile journey. It's a romantic jaunt that recalls the grand days of train travel. Once loaded, the train departs Cedar Park and heads toward Burnet, where passengers have time to shop and dine.

The 143-ton engine that powers the tourist train was constructed by the American Locomotive Company in Dunkirk, New York. For over four decades Southern Pacific Engine No. 786 powered both passenger and freight trains, chugging through Texas and Louisiana, until its retirement in 1956. In 1989, a group of train buffs took on the task of restoring the engine, and in less than two years the former relic was ready to roll once again.

Soon 1920s passenger cars, formerly of the Pennsylvania Railroad, were added and the *Hill Country Flyer* took off, again transporting passengers down the line. Today coach cars plus privately owned first-class cars give travelers a chance to travel in style. The most romantic ride is in first-class aboard Pullman cars with private compartments and an elegant lounge serving complimentary snacks and beverages.

Arrive early in Cedar Park for a visit to Hill Country Cellars (512-259-2000), north of the train stop on US 183. This vineyard produces a Chardonnay, a Hill Country Blush, and a Cabernet Sauvignon.

For More Information: To find up-to-the-minute information about the peak season for the flowers or to learn where the largest fields of flowers have been spotted, call the Wildflower Hotline, (512) 370-0000, ext. 9500. This five-minute recording highlights the best spots for wildflower viewing throughout the state of Texas.

A brochure about the Bluebonnet Trail activities is published by the Lake Buchanan/Inks Lake Chamber of Commerce, P.O. Box 282, Buchanan Dam, TX 78609, or call (512) 793-2803.

Other Wildflower Festivals:

Dallas: Celebrate the colors of spring at Dallas Blooms in the Dallas Arboretum and Botanical Showcase. The 66-acre garden is the largest display of spring color in the Southwest. Early March. (214) 3127-8263.

Houston: Follow the River Oaks Azalea Trail for a peek at blooms in private yards, the River Oaks Garden Club Civic Building and Gardens, and Bayou Bend House and Gardens. Early March. (713) 523-2483.

Independence: Just south of College Station, this town celebrates the Fall Festival of Roses in early November. Experts talk about roses and other plants and the Antique Rose Emporium offers tours of their over 200 varieties of blooms. Early November. (409) 836-5548.

Palestine: Ride the Rusk Railroad to Palestine, then enjoy a look at blooming dogwood trees, enjoy a trolley bus tour, and more. Late March to early April. (903) 729-7275 or 729-6066.

Tyler: East Texas is alive with blooms during the Azalea and Spring Flower Trail. A seven-mile self-guided trail follows the blooms through historic neighborhoods. The weekend fun continues with an antique show, arts and crafts fair, quilt show, and more. Late March to early April. (903) 592-1661 or (800) 235-5712.

In the fall, lovers enjoy the Texas Rose Festival with garden tours, a rose parade, queen's tea, symphony in the park, rose field tours, and more. Mid-October. (903) 597-3130.

CHRISTMAS FESTIVALS

Looking for Christmas? Don't search the horizon for a man in a red suit or for eight tiny reindeer. Look for the Pony Express rider. The Alamo–La Bahia corridor, a 90-mile stretch from San Antonio to Goliad, heralds Christmas in true Texas style with an annual **Christmas Along the Corridor** celebration. This event combines history and Christmas joy in a festival that's as unique as the region itself.

"We've been doing this for about seven years," says Burma Hyde, tourism development coordinator for the Alamo Area Council of Governments. "The idea was to use historically focused tourism for economic development. With 'Christmas Along the Corridor,' we are trying to draw attention to the history, beauty, and the heritage of the area." The result is a festival that features **Pony Express Christmas Couriers,** horseback riders who gallop from town to town spreading the spirit of Christmas.

On the first Saturday of December, festivities begin in Goliad at 8 a.m. with the departure of the Pony Express riders from **Presidio La Bahia.** After the riders depart, plan to stay to take a look at this fascinating landmark. Located on US 183 south of the San Antonio River, the Presidio holds many titles: it is the oldest fort in the West, one of few sites west of the Mississippi that was active in the American Revolution, the only fully restored Spanish *presidio,* and the only Texas Revolution site with its original appearance intact. While you're here, visit the fort chapel, built in the Spanish colonial style.

From the Presidio, the riders travel to **Goliad's Courthouse Square** for the reading of a Governor's Proclamation marking the start of the festivities. Following the proclamation, the riders split up along three routes that wind through this historic region and into the city of **San Antonio.** Like the Pony Express riders of yesteryear, these hand off their duties to the next rider as they travel.

Riders continue spreading Christmas cheer as they travel to the communities of **Runge, Helena, Panna Maria, Cestohowa, Stocksdale, Sutherland Springs, La Vernia, Kenedy, Karnes City, Hobson, Falls City, Poth, Floresville, Pleasanton, Poteet,** and **Elmendorf.** Many of these communities set up special Pony Express postal cancellation stations. Bring along your Christmas cards for a special cancellation commemorating the festival.

Although the arrival of the Pony Express riders is the most unique element of this celebration, festivities continue throughout the day even after the riders have continued down the road. In Goliad, visitors enjoy craft booths, food, live music, and an evening **Las Posadas** procession from the Courthouse Square to Presidio La Bahia.

Just down the road in **Panna Maria,** which means "Virgin Mary" in Polish, guests can enjoy walking tours of the historic church, museum, and village. It's appropriate that this historic burg is part of the Christmas corridor festivities, because its very roots date back to a Christmas over a century ago. After a nine-week voyage from Poland to Galveston, 100 families rented Mexican carts to transport their farm tools and bedding as well as the cross from their parish church. They made the difficult journey to Central Texas on foot, finally stopping at the hillside that overlooks the San Antonio River and Cibolo Creek. The day was December 24, 1854, and the pioneers offered a midnight mass beneath one of the large hilltop oaks. The site later became Panna Maria.

After a look at the location where those early pioneers built their first church, visitors can shop for locally made crafts or enjoy Polish sausage cooked on-site at the Panna Maria **Visitors' Center.** Evening festivities include a lighting ceremony, evening mass, and singing of Polish Christmas carols.

Floresville residents and guests celebrate the day with "Christmas in the Country." A Las Posadas procession, Christmas concert, tree lighting, and hayride to view the colorful holiday lights are followed by an evening of holiday foods, the reading of "Cowboy's Night Before Christmas," and caroling.

The festivities reach a peak with the arrival of over 100 Pony Express riders into **San Antonio.** Following an honor guard bearing the six flags of the corridor, the riders gallop through the southeast gates of the **Mis-**

sion San Juan bearing the Governor's Proclamation. Following the proclamation of the start of the Christmas season, the mission celebrates with period crafts and foods, and Native American dances and music, all representing mission life during the 18th century.

F Y I 〜

For More Information: Call the Alamo Area Council of Governments at (210) 225-5201.

Other Christmas Festivals:

Central Texas: Enjoy small town warmth at the Christmas Stroll on Georgetown's Courthouse Square. December brings the annual Holiday Home Tour. A half dozen residences, all listed on the National Register of Historic Places, open their doors to visitors. (800) GEO-TOWN.

East Texas: Take a romantic Candlelight Tour in Jefferson for two weekends in early December. For information, call the Marion County Chamber of Commerce at (903) 665-2672.

Six million lights illuminate the town of Marshall during the Wonderland of Lights, one of the brightest events in Texas. Over 3,500 businesses and homes participate in the lighting, and visitors can even take a twirl on an outdoor ice skating rink. (903) 935-7868.

Gulf Coast: Hear ye, hear ye, the ghosts of Christmas past, present, and future are at Dickens on the Strand in Galveston's historic district! This Victorian celebration is one of the most romantic in the state. (409) 765-7834.

North Texas: Enjoy the Fantasy of Lights at Midwestern State University at Wichita Falls, with displays that run throughout the month. (817) 723-2741.

Granbury's historic district is highlighted in the Candlelight Tour, a weekend of horse-drawn carriages and tours of 19th-century homes. (800) 950-2212.

In Dallas, Old City Park comes alive with a candlelight tour. (214) 421-5141.

Enjoy a taste of Christmas past at the Victorian Christmas Celebration in Waxahachie, 30 miles south of Dallas. Held three weekends after Thanksgiving, the festivities include a candlelight historic home tour, carriage rides, a parade, arts and crafts, and plenty of Yuletide fun. (214) 938-7400.

Panhandle: Travel back to the 1800s at the Candlelight Christmas in Lubbock. Lanterns and *luminarias* light the path at the Heritage Center as visitors stroll between the historic structures and enjoy period music and a look at ranch life portrayed by costumed docents. (806) 742-0500.

South Texas: In San Antonio, Fiesta de las Luminarias illuminates the River Walk with thousands of little candles in sand-weighted paper bags. During the Holiday River Festival, the River Walk is also transformed into a Christmas wonderland with hundreds of thousands of tiny lights. On the lighting night following Thanksgiving, the river hosts a floating parade. But the most moving event is Las Posadas, a beautiful ceremony dramatizing Joseph and Mary's search for an inn, with costumed children leading a procession down the River Walk. Holiday songs ring out in both English and Spanish. (800) 447-3372.

West Texas: View the lights of El Paso and Juárez from atop Mt. Franklin, part of the Christmas Trolley Tour of Lights in El Paso. The two-hour tour travels through neighborhoods filled with caroling and Christmas lights. (915) 544-0062.

Visit a pioneer fort decked up with holiday cheer, frontier style, during Christmas at Old Fort Concho in San Angelo. Dine on chuck-wagon fare, listen to cowboy poetry, and cuddle under a sea of stars. (915) 657-4441.

APPENDIX: TEXAS
PASSPORT ADVENTURES

If the two of you enjoy eco-tourism in any form—outdoor photography, naturalist studies, fly fishing, mountain biking, or water sports—Texas has got a trip for you.

The Texas Parks and Wildlife Department recently instituted the first program of its kind in the nation. Working with tour operators, travel agents, private landowners, and private industry, the Texas Parks and Wildlife Department has developed a program of nature tourism that encompasses the entire state.

The result is "Texas Passport Adventures," a series of guided tours that provide outdoor adventure, historic and cultural jaunts, and a look at nature from the eyes of experts. Most trips are three-day, two-night journeys, and all-inclusive, offering meals, lodging, on-site transportation, guide services, and interpretive programs for a single price.

Comfort levels depend on individual tours. If you're looking for luxury, enjoy a historic B&B on the Castroville tour or try the legendary YO Ranch in Kerrville. For a more rustic experience, grab your sleeping bags and trek with llamas into Caprock Canyon or canoe through the shady waters of Caddo Lake.

For a catalog of tours offered through the Texas Passport Adventures program, call (800) 841-6547, or check out the Texas Parks and Wildlife Department page on the World Wide Web (http://www.tpwd.state.tx.us).

INDEX OF
PLACE NAMES

ABOUT THE AUTHORS

John Bigley and Paris Permenter are a husband-wife team of travel writers. Longtime Texas residents, they make their home in the Hill Country west of Austin.

John and Paris write frequently about Texas and other destinations for numerous magazines and newspapers. Their articles and photos have appeared in *Reader's Digest, Texas Highways, Austin American-Statesman, San Antonio Express-News, Dallas Morning News,* and many other publications. They also write a monthly column on Texas travel for San Antonio's *Fiesta* magazine, and they are the Texas editors of *Fine Travel,* an on-line magazine on the World Wide Web.

John and Paris's other books include *Day Trips From San Antonio and Austin,* now in its second edition, and *The Alamo City Guide,* both published by Two Lane Press. They are also the authors of *Texas Barbecue,* named Best Regional Book by the Mid-America Publishers Association and published by Pig Out Publications of Kansas City.

Both Paris and John are members of the American Society of Journalists and Authors. John is a member of Outdoor Writers Association of America, and Paris is a member of the Society of American Travel Writers, the most prestigious organization for professional travel journalists.

ORDER FORM

❦

ORDER DIRECT–CALL (800) 877-3119 or FAX (816) 531-6113

Please rush the following book(s) to me:

___ copy(s) **TEXAS GETAWAYS FOR TWO** for $14.95

___ copy(s) **DAY TRIPS FROM SAN ANTONIO AND AUSTIN** for $11.95

___ copy(s) **DAY TRIPS FROM KANSAS CITY** for $10.95

___ copy(s) **DAY TRIPS FROM NASHVILLE** for $9.95

___ copy(s) **THE ALAMO CITY GUIDE** for $9.95

___ copy(s) **DALLAS CUISINE** for $14.95

___ copy(s) **SAN ANTONIO CUISINE** for $14.95

___ copy(s) **TEXAS BARBECUE** for $14.95

Add shipping/handling as follows: 1–2 books = $3.95; 3–5 books = $6.00

METHOD OF PAYMENT

___ Enclosed is my check for $_____ (payable to *Two Lane Press, Inc.*)

___ Please charge to my credit card: _____VISA _____ MasterCard

Acct. # _____

Signature _____

SHIP TO: _____ **GIFT/SHIP TO:**_____

_____ _____

_____ _____

_____ _____

_____ _____

_____ _____

MAIL COMPLETED ORDER FORM TO:

Two Lane Press, Inc. • 4245 Walnut Street • Kansas City, MO 64111